THRIVE ... THE YEAR OF THE SNAKE

Chinese Zodiac Horoscope 2025

Linda Dearsley

BENNION KEARNY

Published in 2024 by Bennion Kearny

ISBN: 978-1-915855-33-6

Linda Dearsley has asserted her right under the Copyright, Designs and Patents Act, 1988 to be identified as the author of this book.

Copyright 2024. All Rights Reserved. No part of this publication may be reproduced, stored in a retrieval system, or transmitted in any form or by any means, electronic, mechanical, photocopying, recording or otherwise, without the prior permission of the publisher.

Bennion Kearny does not have any control over, or any responsibility for, any author or third-party websites mentioned in or on this publication.

A CIP catalogue record for this book is available from the British Library.

This book is sold subject to the condition that it shall not, by way of trade or otherwise, be lent, re-sold, hired out or otherwise circulated without the publisher's prior consent in any form of binding or cover other than that in which it is published and without a similar condition including this condition being imposed on the subsequent purchaser.

TABLE OF CONTENTS

CHAPTER 1: SUCCESS IN THE YEAR OF THE SNAKE 1
Welcome the Snake 1
   Team Efficient 2
   So, What Just Happened? 2
   Time to Chill. 3
   Going Green 3
   But isn't Wood Brown? 4
   Becoming a Snake Charmer 4
   Avoiding the Fangs 4
   Winning at Snakes & Ladders 5
   A Snake by Any Other Name 5
   Meet the Groovy Green Snake of 1965 – Too Cool for School ... 6
   Love Me Do 6
   All You Need is Love 7
   And the Bands Played On 7
   Hollywood Wants a Slice of the Action 8
   Mini-skirts and Mini-models 8
   The Baby Doll Is Born 9
   Protestors on the March 9
   Scandal and Mystery 9
   Reaching for The Sky 10
   A Brave New World 10
   Here Comes The Future 11
Meet the Glorious Green Snake of 2025 11
   Bigger Than The Whole Sky 12
   Medical Breakthroughs 12
   Wheels Within Wheels 13

The Snake and The White House 13
On the March Again 14
Technology Rules 14
Think Gorgeous 15
But Finally… 15
Why is the Year called Snake? 15
How to Succeed in 2025 18
Find Your Chinese Astrology Sign 18
And there's More to it Than That… 18
The Meaning of Your Chinese Numbers 22

CHAPTER 2: THE SNAKE 24

Will 2025 be a Glorious Year for the Snake? 24
The Wonder of Being a Snake 26
The Snake Home 27
Being Friends with the Snake 27
Snake Superpowers 28
Best Jobs for Snake 28
Perfect Partners 28
Snake Love 2025 Style 30
Secrets of Success in 2025 31
The Snake Year at a Glance 32

CHAPTER 3: THE HORSE 34

Will 2025 be a Glorious Year for the Horse? 34
The Wonder of Being a Horse 36
The Horse Home 37
Being Friends with the Horse 37
Horse Superpowers 38
Best Jobs for Horse 38
Perfect Partners 38

Horse Love 2025 Style 41
Secrets of Success in 2025 41
The Horse Year at a Glance 42

CHAPTER 4: THE GOAT 44
Will 2025 be a Glorious Year for the Goat? 44
The Wonder of Being a Goat 46
The Goat home 47
Being Friends with the Goat 48
Goat Superpowers 48
Best Jobs for Goat 48
Perfect Partners 49
Goat Love 2025 Style 51
Secrets of Success in 2025 51
The Goat Year at a Glance 52

CHAPTER 5: THE MONKEY 54
Will 2025 be a Glorious Year for the Monkey? 54
The Wonder of Being a Monkey 56
The Monkey Home 57
Being Friends with the Monkey 57
Monkey Superpowers 57
Best Jobs 2025 58
Perfect Partners 58
Monkey Love 2025 Style 60
Secrets of Success in 2025 61
The Monkey Year at a Glance 61

CHAPTER 6: THE ROOSTER 63
Will 2025 be a Golden Year for the Rooster? 63
The Wonder of Being a Rooster 65

The Rooster Home..66
Being Friends with the Rooster..66
Rooster Superpowers..66
Best Jobs for Rooster 2025..67
Perfect Partners..67
Rooster Love 2025 Style..69
Secrets of Success in 2025..70
The Rooster Year at a Glance..70

CHAPTER 7: THE DOG..72
Will 2025 be a Glorious Year for the Dog?...72
The Wonder of Being a Dog..74
The Dog Home...75
Being Friends with the Dog...75
Dog Superpowers...76
Best Jobs for Dog..76
Perfect Partners..76
Dog Love 2025 Style...79
Secrets of Success in 2025..79
The Dog Year at a Glance...80

CHAPTER 8: THE PIG..82
Will 2025 be a Glorious Year for the Pig?..82
The Wonder of Being a Pig...84
The Pig Home..85
Being Friends with the Pig..85
Pig Superpowers..86
Best Jobs for Pig...86
Perfect Partners...86
Pig Love 2025 Style..88
Secrets of Success in 2025...89

The Pig Year at a Glance..89

CHAPTER 9: THE RAT 91
Will 2025 be a Glorious Year for the Rat?.....................................91
The Wonder of Being a Rat 93
The Rat Home..94
Being Friends with the Rat...95
Rat Superpowers 95
Best Jobs for Rats in 2025 95
Perfect Partners 2025 95
Rat Love 2025 Style 98
Secrets of Success in 2025 99
The Rat Year at a Glance...99

CHAPTER 10: THE OX..101
Will 2025 be a Glorious year for the Ox? 101
The Wonder of Being an Ox 103
The Ox Home...104
Being Friends with the Ox 105
Ox Superpowers 105
Best Jobs for Ox 2025...105
Perfect Partners..105
Ox Love 2025 Style 108
Secrets of Success in 2025 108
The Ox Year at a Glance...109

CHAPTER 11: THE TIGER 111
Will 2025 be a Glorious Year for the Tiger?................................111
The Wonder of Being a Tiger...113
The Tiger Home 114
Being Friends with the Tiger..115

Tiger Superpowers 115
Best Jobs for Tiger in 2025 115
Perfect Partners 115
Tiger Love 2025 Style 118
Secrets of Success in 2025 118
The Tiger Year at a Glance 119

CHAPTER 12: THE RABBIT 121

Will 2025 be a Glorious Year for the Rabbit? 121
The Wonder of Being a Rabbit 123
The Rabbit Home 124
Being Friends with the Rabbit 124
Rabbit Superpowers 125
Best Jobs for Rabbits 2025 125
Perfect Partners 125
Rabbit Love 2025 Style 127
Secrets of Success in 2025 128
The Rabbit Year at a Glance 129

CHAPTER 13: THE DRAGON 131

Will 2025 be a Glorious Year for the Dragon? 131
The Wonder of Being a Dragon 133
The Dragon Home 134
Being Friends with the Dragon 135
Dragon Superpowers 135
Best Jobs for Dragon 2025 135
Perfect Partners 136
Dragon Love 2025 Style 138
Secrets of Success in 2025 138
The Dragon Year at a Glance 139

CHAPTER 14: BUT THEN THERE'S SO MUCH MORE TO YOU 141

Your Outer Animal – (Birth Year | Creates Your First Impression) 141

Your Inner Animal – (Birth Month | The Private You) 142

    Month of Birth - Your Inner Animal 142

Your Secret Animal – (Birth Hour | The Still, Small Voice Within) 143

    Hours of Birth – Your Secret Animal 143

CHAPTER 15: IN YOUR ELEMENT 145

Metal 149

Water 149

Wood 150

Fire 150

Earth 151

Yin and Yang 152

Friendly Elements 153

Unfriendly Elements 154

CHAPTER 16: WESTERN HOROSCOPES AND CHINESE HOROSCOPES – THE LINK 155

Snake 156

    Aries Snake 156

    Taurus Snake 156

    Gemini Snake 156

    Cancer Snake 156

    Leo Snake 157

    Virgo Snake 157

    Libra Snake 157

    Scorpio Snake 157

  Sagittarius Snake 158

  Capricorn Snake 158

  Aquarius Snake 158

  Pisces Snake 158

Horse 159

  Aries Horse 159

  Taurus Horse 159

  Gemini Horse 159

  Cancer Horse 159

  Leo Horse 159

  Virgo Horse 160

  Libra Horse 160

  Scorpio Horse 160

  Sagittarius Horse 160

  Capricorn Horse 161

  Aquarius Horse 161

  Pisces Horse 161

Goat 161

  Aries Goat 161

  Taurus Goat 161

  Gemini Goat 162

  Cancer Goat 162

  Leo Goat 162

  Virgo Goat 162

  Libra Goat 163

  Scorpio Goat 163

  Sagittarius Goat 163

  Capricorn Goat 163

  Aquarius Goat 163

  Pisces Goat 164

Monkey 164
    Aries Monkey 164
    Taurus Monkey 164
    Gemini Monkey 164
    Cancer Monkey 164
    Leo Monkey 165
    Virgo Monkey 165
    Libra Monkey 165
    Scorpio Monkey 165
    Sagittarius Monkey 165
    Capricorn Monkey 166
    Aquarius Monkey 166
    Pisces Monkey 166
Rooster 166
    Aries Rooster 166
    Taurus Rooster 166
    Gemini Rooster 167
    Cancer Rooster 167
    Leo Rooster 167
    Virgo Rooster 167
    Libra Rooster 167
    Scorpio Rooster 168
    Sagittarius Rooster 168
    Capricorn Rooster 168
    Aquarius Rooster 168
    Pisces Rooster 168
Dog 169
    Aries Dog 169
    Taurus Dog 169
    Gemini Dog 169

 Cancer Dog 169

 Leo Dog 169

 Virgo Dog 170

 Libra Dog 170

 Scorpio Dog 170

 Sagittarius Dog 170

 Capricorn Dog 170

 Aquarius Dog 171

 Pisces Dog 171

Pig 171

 Aries Pig 171

 Taurus Pig 171

 Gemini Pig 171

 Cancer Pig 172

 Leo Pig 172

 Virgo Pig 172

 Libra Pig 172

 Scorpio Pig 172

 Sagittarius Pig 173

 Capricorn Pig 173

 Aquarius Pig 173

 Pisces Pig 173

Rat 173

 Aries Rat 173

 Taurus Rat 174

 Gemini Rat 174

 Cancer Rat 174

 Leo Rat 175

 Virgo Rat 175

 Libra Rat 175

Scorpio Rat 175

Sagittarius Rat 176

Capricorn Rat 176

Aquarius Rat 176

Pisces Rat 177

Ox 177

Aries Ox 177

Taurus Ox 177

Gemini Ox 177

Cancer Ox 178

Leo Ox 178

Virgo Ox 178

Libra Ox 179

Scorpio Ox 179

Sagittarius Ox 179

Capricorn Ox 180

Aquarius Ox 180

Pisces Ox 180

Tiger 181

Aries Tiger 181

Taurus Tiger 181

Gemini Tiger 181

Cancer Tiger 181

Leo Tiger 181

Virgo Tiger 182

Libra Tiger 182

Scorpio Tiger 182

Sagittarius Tiger 183

Capricorn Tiger 183

Aquarius Tiger 183

Pisces Tiger 183
Rabbit 184
    Aries Rabbit 184
    Taurus Rabbit 184
    Gemini Rabbit 184
    Cancer Rabbit 184
    Leo Rabbit 185
    Virgo Rabbit 185
    Libra Rabbit 185
    Scorpio Rabbit 185
    Sagittarius Rabbit 185
    Capricorn Rabbit 186
    Aquarius Rabbit 186
    Pisces Rabbit 186
Dragon 186
    Aries Dragon 186
    Taurus Dragon 187
    Gemini Dragon 187
    Cancer Dragon 187
    Leo Dragon 187
    Virgo Dragon 188
    Libra Dragon 188
    Scorpio Dragon 188
    Sagittarius Dragon 188
    Capricorn Dragon 189
    Aquarius Dragon 189
    Pisces Dragon 189

CHAPTER 17: CREATE A WONDERFUL YEAR 190

CHAPTER 1: SUCCESS IN THE YEAR OF THE SNAKE

Welcome the Snake

Great news! For everyone who reckons it's time for change – your wish is granted!

Here it comes, shimmying over the horizon on January the 29th, wrapped around the iridescent jade-green scales of the Snake.

Wisdom of the Snake

> A person can change his future merely by changing his attitude.
>
> **Oprah Winfrey**
> (1954 Water Snake)

Yes, 2025 is the year of the glorious Green Wood Snake. You might like to slip into something elegant yet subtly sexy to welcome the serpent's arrival because we're dealing with understated yet very chic energy here. Loud, vulgar displays will be ignored or treated with disdain. Think classy, and you won't go far wrong.

As the wild, colourful – some might say brash – exuberance of the departing Dragon of 2024 disappears into the night, the world is bathed in a quieter, enigmatic, almost mysterious new vibe. This could come as a relief to nervous types, but don't be fooled.

Traditionally, the Snake is regarded as a symbol of renewal and rebirth – thanks to its strange ability to shed its skin and emerge, apparently remade. So we could be looking at change here, with a capital C.

As 2025 unfolds, the Snake's lustrous coils will encircle the year, imperceptibly influencing everything, until the serpent finally glides away on February the 10th 2026, leaving everything utterly altered.

Team Efficient

The Chinese often refer to the Snake as the Little Dragon, but this is perhaps to underestimate the Snake. Snake is far more than just a pale imitation of its mighty cousin. The Snake possesses a silent, almost hypnotic power all its own. Where the Dragon rushes around, making grand gestures and demanding maximum razzmatazz at every turn, the Snake lounges inscrutably on the sidelines, making seemingly little effort. Yet, after a while, it turns out a great deal has been accomplished, although no one can quite see how.

The Snake is literally the Yin to the Dragon's Yang. The two complement each other perfectly.

So, What Just Happened?

The Dragon of 2024, as promised, brought in a typically dynamic and action-packed year. We had the Paris Olympics, the Paralympics, the

European Cup tournament, several dramatic political elections and the phenomenal Taylor Swift world tour. On the less positive side, there was an assassination attempt on a former US president, the decline of the sitting president, plus escalations to the wars in Gaza and Ukraine.

If it sometimes seemed like we were going through one drama after another – that's because we were. Dragon years are about action and growth, but always in the hope of shaking things up to build a brighter, better future. Those endless showers of Olympic medals, shiny football trophies, and the soaring fireworks of the Swiftie concerts, inspired millions around the world in true Dragon fashion. The continuation of those pesky wars – well, Dragon would prefer to draw a veil over those. But pace like this, whether good or bad, can't be sustained forever, which is where the Snake comes in.

Time to Chill...

...just don't doze off. Yes, we can look forward to a noticeable toning down of the wild, unruly energy of 2024. Most of us should feel a gentle slowing of pace, a sense of certain pressures being released, and the urgency of some situations fading. Exactly what's needed after the frenetic events of last year. Yet, this is no time to take a long nap. Relax a little, by all means, but keep at least one eye open for unexpected changes – a particular speciality of the Snake.

Snake years always follow Dragon years, and there's a good reason the Snake is often referred to as the aforementioned Little Dragon. The Snake finishes what Dragon started but in a quieter, less obtrusive manner. Changes underway in 2024 – but not completed – won't disappear. Snake will discreetly move in and speed things along.

Never forget that these two, though apparently complete opposites in size and personality, work together as an unofficial team, using different but equally formidable skills to achieve the same goals. Should Dragon's blunt, full-frontal approach fail, Snake's right behind, ready to follow up with a clever ingenuity that may well do the trick.

Going Green

It seems like green has been the spiritual colour of the whole decade so far, but never more so than in 2024, and we can look forward to the same again in 2025.

So why is this year's Snake green? According to Chinese tradition, as well as being ruled by an animal, each year is also influenced by an element, symbolised by a colour. The year's animal arrives dressed in that year's colour, while the year itself takes on the personality of the animal plus the qualities associated with the element.

Green is the colour that symbolises Wood in Chinese lore, and 2025 – like 2024 – is a Wood year, which is why the Snake of 2025 comes in glorious green.

But isn't Wood Brown?

This can be confusing for people in the West. We tend to think of Wood as being brown in colour. But that's because we're thinking of different things. The Chinese Wood element represents not chunky furniture and floorboards or ornamental carvings. That sort of Wood is regarded as merely the end result of the mysterious energy that impels a tiny seed to grow into a towering tree, sprouting millions of green leaves along the way.

Maybe, one Spring long ago in ancient times, a Chinese thinker looked around at the vibrant green shoots bursting out everywhere – from the grass beneath his feet to the tops of the tallest trees – and wondered what amazing force could cause this. It was clearly a very special, life-giving energy, and it came to be known as Wood. Therefore, all growing plant life, from the tiniest blade of grass to the mightiest oak is, to this day, regarded as Wood.

So, Wood years tend to be as welcome as the Spring – for the same reason. They promise a return to the world of colour, growth, and vitality, of optimism and hope. True, Snake years are not as auspicious as Dragon years, but that's partly because the Dragon is the most auspicious of the signs. None of the others can live up to that.

Becoming a Snake Charmer

So, what will the Year of the Snake bring to you? Will you have that serpent bending and swaying and dancing to your tune, beaming golden opportunities and good luck your way? Or will you trip over the slumbering snake hidden in the grass and run screaming from an angry, hissing serpent?

The outcome is not as unpredictable as it might seem. Just like the old Snake charmers of the East, you can learn to beguile your Snake with the right kind of music and turn 2025 into an effortless, magical year.

True, some signs are naturally more on the Snake's wavelength than others and will find it easier to charm favours, but even those signs that tend to be tone-deaf when it comes to Snake's favourite melodies can learn how to improve their chances.

Avoiding the Fangs

One thing to bear in mind, though – and unlike some of the zodiac creatures such as the cuddly Rabbit and the lovable Pig – is that the

Snake is a particularly tricky character. Sleepy and serene one minute, hissing and spitting venom without warning the next. Snake years tend to take on the same quality. One moment, you're cruising along, everything's going well, and you're making great progress. The next, a crisis blows up out of nowhere, and suddenly, you're knocked sideways.

Snake years can be seriously unpredictable, yet according to Chinese lore, you don't have to feel helpless.

Winning at Snakes & Ladders

The secret is deceptively simple. Once you understand what lies beneath the Snake's inscrutable exterior, how it reacts to your personal sign, and what kind of things upset it, the way ahead becomes clearer.

For a start, it's no good to assume that what worked well for you last year will be just as successful in 2025. Clever types will alter their strategy to suit the new energy. Bold, audacious plans that won applause in Dragon's reign could suddenly look slap-dash and rather tacky to the discriminating Snake. Applying the same actions in 2025 could send you shooting straight down a ladder.

Yet, if you adapt and rework your ideas to suit the Snake's preferences, you could find yourself wafting rapidly to success.

A Snake by Any Other Name

Another point to bear in mind is that though all Snake years share a basic 'snakeyness', zodiac Snakes come in five different varieties – breeds as it were. And each has its own subtle personality variation. In coming years, we'll meet the Scarlet Fire Snake, the Brown Earth Snake, and – if we live long enough – the Golden Metal Snake and the Blue Water Snake because each serpent gets the chance to rule just once every 60 years. But right now, 2025 belongs to the Green Wood Snake and we won't see it's like again until 2085, so we need to make the most of it.

This Snake, exuding Wood energy like last year's Dragon, is just as devoted to expansion and growth and new directions as its fiery cousin but prefers a more controlled, orderly approach. Not as theatrical perhaps, but it has a particular fondness for music and the more refined arts.

Change is the law of life.

John F. Kennedy
(1917 Fire Snake)

Wisdom of the Snake

And we can get a sneak preview of what might be in store for us in 2025 by checking out what happened *the last time* the Green Wood Snake took charge of proceedings – six whole decades ago, way back in 1965.

Meet the Groovy Green Snake of 1965 – Too Cool for School

By the time the Groovy Green Snake of '65 boogied in on the heels of the departing Green Dragon, bringing a second blast of the spring-like Wood energy introduced by Dragon, the youth culture sweeping the world under its beneficial influence had taken firm root and was blossoming fast.

It seemed that musicians were especially favoured by the Snake. The Beatles, who'd been the sensation of '64, continued to enjoy good fortune.

Love Me Do

Success heaped on success for the band. Hit followed hit. The Fab Four found time to tour Europe, the UK, and the USA, where they made history by staging the world's first open-air stadium concert at the Shea Stadium in New York before a crowd of 55,000.

In between tours, they managed to film and release their second movie, Help, which was given a Royal premiere attended by Princess Margaret and the Earl of Snowden. And, in October, they were invited to Buckingham Palace to receive MBEs (Member of the British Empire) from the Queen. This honour was controversial – until then, the medals were usually awarded to military heroes, politicians, and dignitaries. Apparently, some previous recipients were so incensed at this 'downgrading' of the honour that they returned their medals in disgust.

Undaunted, the Beatles sailed on.

All You Need is Love

The Fab Four's personal lives were going just as well. Ringo married his long-term girlfriend Maureen on February the 11th, just a week into the Snake year, and by September, their first child, Zak, was born.

Inspired, George Harrison proposed to Patti Boyd, the girl he'd met while making the Beatles' first film, A Hard Day's Night, the year before. They planned their wedding over the Christmas break and tied the knot just as the Snake departed on January the 21st 1966.

Meanwhile, Paul McCartney enjoyed several holidays with his long-term girlfriend, actress Jane Asher; and John Lennon, already married to his wife Cynthia, passed his driving test and published his second volume of eccentric wordplay and drawings, A Spaniard in the Works.

Wisdom of the Snake

> If you want to keep your memories, you first have to live them.
>
> **Bob Dylan**
> (1941 Metal Snake)

And the Bands Played On

It wasn't just the Beatles. Music was everywhere in 1965, and there was something for everyone. The soundtrack to the hit musical Mary Poppins was the top-selling album of the year and singer/actress Julie Andrews was particularly blessed. She won a Golden Globe, followed a few months later by an Oscar for her performance as Mary Poppins. In March, her follow-up movie, The Sound of Music, burst onto cinema screens. At first, the critics were unenthusiastic, finding the story too 'sugar coated' for their taste, but audiences loved its family-friendly theme and beautiful setting. The Sound of Music went on to win five Oscars and has been delighting audiences ever since.

Meanwhile, the not-so-family-friendly Rolling Stones had a smash hit with I Can't Get No Satisfaction, and amongst other subjects, Mick Jagger was busy writing Mother's Little Helper about tranquiliser drugs.

Hollywood Wants a Slice of the Action

Sensing the music business was now a gold mine, Hollywood put out an ad for four young men interested in forming a pop group for a fictional TV show, inadvertently creating the world's first Boy Band in the process. The Monkees soon leapt from TV and morphed into a real band, with British actor/singer Davy Jones as the lead vocalist.

They may have been a manufactured band, but The Monkees were such a rapid success that they caused another aspiring young British singer – also named David Jones – to change his name to avoid confusion. That year, David Jones became David Bowie. He released his first David Bowie single on January the 14th 1966 – just in time to capture some magical Snake luck before the year ended a week later.

And at the other end of the scale, a youthful tenor named Luciano Pavarotti made his debut at La Scala in a revival of La bohème. He would go far.

Mini-skirts and Mini-models

The other remarkable thing about Snakes is the way they can shed their skin and reappear with a fresh new look, so it's no surprise Snake years often herald an emphasis on clothes and changing fashion.

1965 was particularly revolutionary. It's unclear who invented the mini skirt as hemlines had been inching up for several years, but in 1964, Paris couturier André Courrèges caused a stir with a collection featuring short skirts and space-age dresses. Inspired by Courrèges and also the way the young girls around her Chelsea studio dressed, British designer Mary Quant created a range of simple designs reminiscent of the schoolgirl pinafore, with hemlines firmly fixed above the knee.

The look demanded long, slim legs and a coltish, youthful figure. It was a fashion made for the young. Perfect for teenagers, hopeless for their mothers. Mary said she called her design the 'mini-skirt' after the trendiest car of the moment, the Mini (the previous year, the Mini Cooper had won the prestigious Monte Carlo Rally and did so again in '65).

Shortly afterwards, Jean Shrimpton, the top model of the day, shocked the world by turning up at Australia's swanky Melbourne Cup Carnival wearing a brief, white shift dress, a scandalous four inches above the knee. She compounded the outrage by failing to add stockings, gloves, or even a hat to her outfit. Such an undergroomed appearance in polite society was judged so disgraceful it made appalled headlines around the globe.

The Baby Doll Is Born

Meanwhile, back in north-west London, apparently unaware of the Shrimpton controversy, a 15-year-old schoolgirl was hoping to break into modelling despite weighing only six stone and having legs so thin she was nicknamed Twigs. Unfazed, young Lesley Hornby played around with make-up and often ringed her eyes with dark liner and drew on exaggerated fake lashes beneath her lower lids to recreate the painted face look of her favourite rag doll.

Shortly after her 16th birthday, Lesley treated herself to a haircut at London's fashionable salon, Leonard Lewis. As it happened, the great man himself was looking for volunteers on which to trial his newest style – the pixie crop. Lesley reluctantly agreed to be Leonard's guinea pig and allowed him to chop off her long locks. Hours later, Leonard declared himself so pleased with the boyish result that he had the newly shorn Lesley photographed and displayed the picture in his shop window.

Before the Snake year ended, a passing fashion journalist spotted the striking portrait. She contacted Lesley, organised her own photoshoot with the teenager, ditched the name Lesley for Twiggy, and in the resulting story declared Twiggy – with her mini-skirt perfect legs – as the Face of '66...

The fashion world would never be the same again.

Protestors on the March

In the USA, President Johnson was settling into his first term, while in Britain, the Labour Party's Harold Wilson was finding his feet.

Yet, out in the country, the people (particularly the young) were on the march. More US troops were sent to the war in Vietnam, and 25,000 people marched on Washington in protest. It was the biggest demonstration ever known. Feelings were running just as high down south, triggering three separate civil rights marches. One was led by Martin Luther King, who marched from Selma in Alabama to the state capital, Montgomery, 54 miles away, demanding voting rights for the black population.

The anti-war protestors were to fail in their mission, but the Selma marchers eventually succeeded. On August the 6th, President Johnson signed the historic Voting Rights Act of 1965.

Scandal and Mystery

Meanwhile, over in France, a major scandal was brewing. Moroccan political activist Mehdi Ben Barka, likened in stature to the legendary Che Guevara, was lured to Paris from his home in Geneva, where he was living in exile, for a meeting. Unfortunately for him, when he reached the fashionable Brasserie where the meeting was to take place, French police officers were waiting outside. They bundled him into a car, drove him away, and Ben Barka was never seen again.

It's believed he was driven to a house on the outskirts of Paris, where he was tortured and killed by Moroccan agents. His body has never been found. The ensuing scandal caused a political crisis for French President Charles de Gaulle. The French police, French Intelligence, and even America's CIA and Israel's Mossad were, at various times, mentioned in connection with Ben Barka's kidnap, as well as the Moroccan agents. To this day, the mystery of his disappearance has never been solved.

Reaching for The Sky

Elsewhere, the restless spirit of expansion and exploration mushroomed, epitomised by continued fascination with space and the planets. In February, Russian cosmonaut Alexei Leonov became the first man to walk in space, followed swiftly in June by the USA's Ed White.

Wisdom of the Snake

Anything's possible if you've got enough nerve.

JK Rowling
(1965 Wood Snake)

A month later, the first close-up pictures of Mars were transmitted from Mariner 4 to an astonished world. It seemed as if the planets were almost within our grasp.

And earthbound London, not to be completely outdone, also reached for the sky by opening the futuristic Post Office Tower: a slender spike, not unlike a spaceship on a gantry, itself. It became the tallest building in the city and boasted a revolving restaurant at the top where adventurous visitors could dine in the clouds.

A Brave New World

As the space age flourished, modernisation became the theme of the year. Britain's Met Office, tasked with forecasting the country's weather and often ridiculed for inaccuracies, ditched its old-fashioned ways and brought in new-fangled computers to make their predictions.

In the medical field, Northern Irish cardiologist Frank Pantridge, frustrated at the deadly delay in treating heart attack victims, invented the first portable defibrillator using car batteries. Weighing around 70 kgs, the machine was installed in an ambulance just before the Snake year ended. The results were so encouraging that the idea was adopted around the world. Frank became known as the father of emergency medicine and his concept has been saving lives ever since.

Here Comes The Future

Out in the North Sea, the UK's first oil rig to search for oil and natural gas was conjured up from a converted barge and anchored 47 miles offshore. Named the Sea Gem, it proudly began work in June. By the end of September, it had located a substantial pocket of natural gas beneath the sea bed – enough to power a medium-sized city. Forget outdated coal, the headlines screamed; a golden future of cheap, clean energy had arrived.

But then, in one of those unpredictable twists for which the Snake is famous, disaster struck. On December the 26th, Boxing Day, two of the Sea Gem's ten legs suddenly collapsed without warning, plunging the whole platform into the waves. Thirteen men lost their lives that day.

Meet the Glorious Green Snake of 2025

So, bearing in mind the events that shaped the world the last time the Green Snake took charge, what can we expect from 2025?

Chances are that we'll be aware of a quieter, slower, almost feminine quality in the air after a while. The Dragon may depart with such a flamboyant flounce it could appear at first that nothing much is happening. It's all gone too quiet. Only gradually will it dawn that actually a great deal is going on, but behind the scenes, out of view.

Expect secrets and mysteries, rumours and scandals. The Snake rather encourages digging deep. Gullible types who take everything at face value and can't be bothered to ask questions are likely to lose out big time. Enquiring minds and investigative personalities will be rewarded for their diligence.

Show-offs, big-mouths, and fakes from all walks of life are likely to fall flat on their faces, often very publicly, too. And don't expect them to be reinstated any time soon. The Snake can be very unforgiving.

Bigger Than The Whole Sky

The Snake of '25 is likely to be just as music-loving as the Grandma Green Snake of '65, with female musicians being particularly favoured. Expect new female singers to burst onto the scene, but in the meantime, the Taylor Swift phenomenon is likely to continue and accelerate in unexpected ways.

Interestingly, Taylor Swift is herself a Snake – born in the Earth Snake year of 1989. In 2025, it looks like she'll take the whole world by surprise as she demonstrates her skin-shedding abilities. Expect Taylor to strike out in an exciting, completely different direction.

Wisdom of the Snake

> Anytime someone tells me I can't do something, I want to do it more.
>
> **Taylor Swift**
> (1989 Earth Snake)

Singer/actress Ariana Grande, already enjoying the success of 2024's hit movie Wicked, will repeat her good fortune in 2025 when Wicked: Part 2 reaches the screens and the soundtrack tops the charts.

Watch out, too, for another female artist, not a singer but a writer, Harry Potter creator, JK Rowling. Ms Rowling looks likely to be hitting the headlines in 2025. The renowned author is actually a Green Wood Snake herself, born in the revolutionary year of 1965, and it looks as if she's preparing to shed her old skin in a dramatic way. A reborn Ms Rowling, returning to her birthright, will startle fans by launching a controversial new project – possibly connected to politics or activism. In a mood like this, Ms Rowling really could change the world.

Medical Breakthroughs

The Snake has been connected to medicine and healing since the time of the ancient Greeks, so we can expect companies connected to healthcare and pharmaceuticals to continue to do well.

Despite the fact that Covid has seemingly faded into the background, there's still likely to be a preoccupation with health and health matters in 2025 and an expansion of interest and knowledge on the part of the public. Alternative therapies become ever more sought-after, while medical mistakes and scandals will have the healing Snake hissing with rage. Uncaring or dishonest practitioners can expect no mercy from the furious serpent.

Since we're dealing with the Green Wood Snake here, expect the health-giving properties of the great outdoors, particularly the countryside, to be brought into sharp focus. Also, the beneficial effects of sunshine. Despite years of warnings to avoid too much sun, the Snake loves soaking up the rays as often as possible, so 2025 could find us being encouraged back to our sun loungers.

Professions involved in every aspect of healthcare, therapy, and beauty will flourish under the Snake's benevolent eye.

And, as with the portable defibrillator of 1965, we could see an ingenious medical invention introduced which will go on to transform a particular field and save many lives.

Wheels Within Wheels

Unlike the extrovert Dragon, what you see is definitely not what you get with the Snake. The Snake likes to operate discreetly behind closed doors. The deeper the intrigue, the juicier the scandal, the better Snake likes it. But only as long as the Snake is involved or at least kept informed. Leave the Snake out, attempt to hide the plans, and a vengeful serpent will strike fearlessly when the truth finally emerges.

For this reason, there could be huge upheavals in 2025 when past plots and unsavoury secrets are ruthlessly exposed. Researchers, detectives, investigative journalists, online podcasters, and even amateur sleuths will be aided by the Snake to uncover bad or dishonourable behaviour on every level.

Expect household names, global companies, and even entire governments to come crashing down under the forensic eye of the unblinking serpent.

The Snake and The White House

Of all the intrigue that delights the Snake, perhaps political intrigue is the type the serpent enjoys most. So, it's no coincidence that just nine days before the Snake year beings, the new President of the USA, Donald Trump, is due to be inaugurated on January the 20th 2025, after a year of the most astonishing political turmoil.

Spookily, Donald Trump was born in the year of the Fire Dog in 1946, as were two previous living presidents: Bill Clinton and George W Bush. Even stranger, George W Bush actually won his election in 2000 – a

Dragon year, just like last year, and was inaugurated in the year of the Snake 2001.

Donald Trump can expect a hectic year with many behind-the-scenes secret negotiations and strategies to devise. Chances are he will also encounter much clandestine plotting against him as well as potential backstabbers, but then after the year of the Dragon he's just survived, he's probably well prepared.

Wisdom of the Snake

Intelligence is the ability to adapt to change.

Stephen Hawking
(1942 Metal Snake)

On the March Again

While Wood is associated with growth and expansion, it can also be associated negatively with anger – which might explain the protest marches of 1965. True, there was no shortage of marches in 2024 either, but these mass protests are likely to increase in 2025 under the influence of Wood, and the range of grievances will broaden. Subjects barely mentioned last year will suddenly flare into bitter conflicts, and people will take to the streets.

Violence can't be ruled out, and the abduction or murder of some sort of activist – similar to the Mehdi Ben Barka affair – could leave politicians on the brink.

Technology Rules

And just as in 1965, the world's love affair with technology and space will grow ever stronger. AI will increase its grip and expand into more and more fields. Technological titans such as Elon Musk and Bill Gates will dominate the news.

International space projects are likely to become even more ambitious, along with efforts to make contact with aliens.

And, of course, conspiracy theories will flourish and become ever more outrageous under the influence of the Snake. There's nothing the Snake enjoys more than a good conspiracy.

Think Gorgeous

Artists, designers, and creators of anything beautiful can expect to be blessed with good fortune this year. The Snake adores lovely things and is quite prepared to pay lavishly for them, should they happen to be expensive. Despite the financial difficulties of the past few years, chances are we'll all long for a little luxury in 2025, and some could even get into debt over the strong impulse to splash out. Forget budget holidays and cheap camping trips – they just won't cut it now. 2025 is likely to see the return of the glam five-star break, preferably somewhere hot and exotic – even if it takes all year to pay off the credit card.

But Finally…

Never underestimate the huge significance of the Snake and the effect its skin-shedding powers of transformation could have on 2025. From the beginning of the Great Depression in 1929 to the Attack on Pearl Harbour in 1941, from the fall of Communism in 1989 to the Twin Towers atrocity of 2001 – an extraordinary number of far-reaching, world-shattering events have taken place in Snake years. This is not a coincidence.

Tread carefully…

Wisdom of the Snake

Remember if you ever need a helping hand, it's at the end of your arm.

Audrey Hepburn
(1929 Earth Snake)

Why is the Year called Snake?

According to Chinese folklore, there are many explanations as to why the calendar is divided up the way it is. Perhaps the most popular is the story about the supreme Jade Emperor who lives in heaven. He decided to name each year in honour of a different animal and decreed that a race would be run to decide which animals would be chosen, and the order in which they would appear.

Twelve animals arrived to take part. Actually, in one legend, there were 13, including the Cat, who was a great friend of the Rat at the time. But the Cat was a sleepy creature and asked the Rat to wake him in time for the race. In the excitement (or was it by design?), the Rat forgot and dashed off, leaving the Cat fast asleep. The Cat missed the race and missed out on getting a year dedicated to his name. Which is why cats have hated rats ever since.

The Wily Rat and the Patient Ox

Anyway, as they approached the finish line, the 12 competitors found a wide river blocking their route. The powerful Ox, a strong swimmer, plunged straight in, but the tiny Rat begged to be carried across on his back. Kindly Ox agreed, but when they reached the opposite bank, the wily Rat scampered down Ox's body, jumped off his head and shot across the finish line in first place. Which is why the Rat is the first animal of the Chinese zodiac, followed by the Ox.

The Magnificent Tiger and the Ingenious Rabbit

The muscular Tiger, weighed down by his magnificent coat, arrived in third place, followed by the non-swimming Rabbit, who'd found some rocks downstream and hopped neatly from one to another until it spotted a log floating along and jumped on to be carried safely to dry land.

The Dragon Delayed

The Emperor was surprised to see the Dragon with his great wings, fly in, in fifth place, instead of the expected first. The Dragon explained that while high up in the sky, he saw a village in flames and the people running out of their houses in great distress, so he'd made a detour and employed his rain-making skills (Chinese Dragons can create water as well as fire) to put out the blaze before returning to the race. In some versions of the story, Dragon also adds that as he approached the river, he spotted poor little Rabbit clinging perilously to a log, so Dragon gently blew the log across and watched to see Rabbit safely ashore before flying over himself.

The Shrewd Snake and the Obliging Horse

In sixth place came the Snake. Clever as the Rat, the Snake had wrapped himself around one of the Horse's hooves and hung on while the Horse swam the river. When the Horse climbed ashore, the Snake slithered off, so startling the Horse that it reared up in alarm, allowing the Snake to slide over the finish line ahead of him.

The Three Musketeers: the Goat, the Monkey and the Rooster

The Goat, Monkey, and Rooster arrived next at the river. They spotted some driftwood and rope washed up on the shore, so Monkey deftly lashed them together to make a raft and the three of them hopped aboard and floated across. The Goat jumped off first, swiftly followed by Monkey and Rooster.

The Dallying Dog and the Hungry Pig

They found they'd beaten the Dog, which was unexpected as the Dog was a good swimmer. It turned out the Dog so enjoyed the water, he'd hung around playing in the shallows, emerging only in time to come eleventh. Last of all came the Pig, not the best of swimmers, and further slowed by his decision to pause for a good meal before exerting himself in the current.

The Wheel of the Zodiac is Complete

And so, the wheel of the zodiac was set forevermore, with the Year of the Rat beginning the cycle, followed by the Ox, Tiger, Rabbit, Dragon, Snake, Horse, Goat, Monkey, Rooster, Dog and Pig.

How to Succeed in 2025

So, since 2025 is the Year of the Snake, how will you fare? Does the Snake present your astrological animal with opportunities or challenges? As the fable about how the years got their names shows, every one of the astrological animals is resourceful in its own special way. Faced with the prospect of crossing the river, each successfully made it to the other side, even the creatures that could barely swim.

So, whether your year animal gets on easily with the Green Wood Snake or whether they have to work at their relationship, you can make 2025 a special year to remember.

Chinese Astrology has been likened to a weather forecast. Once you know whether you'll need your umbrella or your suntan lotion, you can step out with confidence and enjoy the trip.

Find Your Chinese Astrology Sign

To find your Chinese sign, just look up your birth year in the table below.

Important note: if you were born in January or February, check the dates of the New Year very carefully. The Chinese New Year follows the lunar calendar and the beginning and end dates are not fixed, but vary each year. If you were born before mid-February, your animal sign might actually be the sign of the previous year. For example, 1980 was the year of the Monkey, but the Chinese New Year began on February 16, so a person born in January or early February 1980 would belong to the year before – the year of the Goat.

And there's More to it Than That...

In case you're saying to yourself, but surely, how can every person born in the same 365 days have the same personality(?) – you're quite right. The birth year is only the beginning.

Your birth year reflects the way others see you and your basic characteristics, but your month and time of birth are also ruled by the celestial animals – probably different animals from the one that dominates your birth year. The personalities of these other animals modify and add talents to those you acquired with your birth year creature.

The 1920s

5 February 1924 – 24 January 1925 | RAT
25 January 1925 – 12 February 1926 | OX
13 February 1926 – 1 February 1927 | TIGER
2 February 1927 – 22 January 1928 | RABBIT

23 January 1928 – 9 February 1929 | DRAGON
10 February 1929 – 29 January 1930 | SNAKE

The 1930s

30 January 1930 – 16 February 1931 | HORSE
17 February 1931 – 5 February 1932 | GOAT
6 February 1932 – 25 January 1933 | MONKEY
26 January 1933 – 13 February 1934 | ROOST5R
14 February 1934 – 3 February 1935 | DOG
4 February 1935 – 23 January 1936 | PIG
24 January 1936 – 10 February 1937 | RAT
11 February 1937 – 30 January 1938 | OX
31 January 1938 – 18 February 1939 | TIGER
19 February 1939 – 7 February 1940 | RABBIT

The 1940s

8 February 1940 – 26 January 1941 | DRAGON
27 January 1941 – 14 February 1942 | SNAKE
15 February 1942 – 4 February 1943 | HORSE
5 February 1943 – 24 January 1944 | GOAT
25 January 1944 – 12 February 1945 | MONKEY
13 February 1945 – 1 February 1946 | ROOSTER
2 February 1946 – 21 January 1947 | DOG
22 January 1947 – 9 February 1948 | PIG
10 February 1948 – 28 January 1949 | RAT
29 January 1949 – 16 February 1950 | OX

The 1950s

17 February 1950 – 5 February 1951 | TIGER
6 February 1951 – 26 January 1952 | RABBIT
27 January 1952 – 13 February 1953 | DRAGON
14 February 1953 – 2 February 1954 | SNAKE
3 February 1954 – 23 January 1955 | HORSE
24 January 1955 – 11 February 1956 | GOAT
12 February 1956 – 30 January 1957 | MONKEY
31 January 1957 – 17 February 1958 | ROOSTER

18 February 1958 – 7 February 1959 | DOG
8 February 1959 – 27 January 1960 | PIG

The 1960s

28 January 1960 – 14 February 1961 | RAT
15 February 1961 – 4 February 1962 | OX
5 February 1962 – 24 January 1963 | TIGER
25 January 1963 – 12 February 1964 | RABBIT
13 February 1964 – 1 February 1965 | DRAGON
2 February 1965 – 20 January 1966 | SNAKE
21 January 1966 – 8 February 1967 | HORSE
9 February 1967 – 29 January 1968 | GOAT
30 January 1968 – 16 February 1969 | MONKEY
17 February 1969 – 5 February 1970 | ROOSTER

The 1970s

6 February 1970 – 26 January 1971 | DOG
27 January 1971 – 14 February 1972 | PIG
15 February 1972 – 2 February 1973 | RAT
3 February 1973 – 22 January 1974 | OX
23 January 1974 – 10 February 1975 | TIGER
11 February 1975 – 30 January 1976 | RABBIT
31 January 1976 – 17 February 1977 | DRAGON
18 February 1977 – 6 February 1978 | SNAKE
7 February 1978 – 27 January 1979 | HORSE
28 January 1979 – 15 February 1980 | GOAT

The 1980s

16 February 1980 – 4 February 1981 | MONKEY
5 February 1981 – 24 January 1982 | ROOSTER
25 January 1982 – 12 February 1983 | DOG
13 February 1983 – 1 February 1984 | PIG
2 February 1984 – 19 February 1985 | RAT
20 February 1985 – 8 February 1986 | OX
9 February 1986 – 28 January 1987 | TIGER
29 January 1987 – 16 February 1988 | RABBIT

17 February 1988 – 5 February 1989 | DRAGON
6 February 1989 – 26 January 1990 | SNAKE

The 1990s
27 January 1990 – 14 February 1991 | HORSE
15 February 1991 – 3 February 1992 | GOAT
4 February 1992 – 22 January 1993 | MONKEY
23 January 1993 – 9 February 1994 | ROOSTER
10 February 1994 – 30 January 1995 | DOG
31 January 1995 – 18 February 1996 | PIG
19 February 1996 – 7 February 1997 | RAT
8 February 1997 – 27 January 1998 | OX
28 January 1998 – 5 February 1999 | TIGER
6 February 1999 – 4 February 2000 | RABBIT

The 2000s
5 February 2000 – 23 January 2001 | DRAGON
24 January 2001 – 11 February 2002 | SNAKE
12 February 2002 – 31 January 2003 | HORSE
1 February 2003 – 21 January 2004 | GOAT
22 January 2004 – 8 February 2005 | MONKEY
9 February 2005 – 28 January 2006 | ROOSTER
29 January 2006 – 17 February 2007 | DOG
18 February 2007 – 6 February 2008 | PIG
7 February 2008 – 25 January 2009 | RAT
26 January 2009 – 13 February 2010 | OX

The 2010s
14 February 2010 – 2 February 2011 | TIGER
3 February 2011 – 22 January 2012 | RABBIT
23 January 2012 – 9 February 2013 | DRAGON
10 February 2013 – 30 January 2014 | SNAKE
31 January 2014 – 18 February 2015 | HORSE
19 February 2015 – 7 February 2016 | GOAT
8 February 2016 – 27 January 2017 | MONKEY
28 January 2017 – 15 February 2018 | ROOSTER

16 February 2018 – 4 February 2019 | DOG
5 February 2019 – 24 January 2020 | PIG

The 2020s

25 January 2020 – 11 February 2021 | RAT
12 February 2021 – 31 January 2022 | OX
1 February 2022 – 21 January 2023 | TIGER
22 January 2023 – 9 February 2024 | RABBIT
10 February 2024 – 28 January 2025 | DRAGON
29 January 2025 – 16 February 2026 | SNAKE
17 February 2026 – 5 February 2027 | HORSE
6 February 2027 – 25 January 2028 | GOAT
26 January 2028 – 12 February 2029 | MONKEY
13 February 2029 – 2 February 2030 | ROOSTER
3 February 2030 - 22 January 2031 DOG

The Meaning of Your Chinese Numbers

Across the following zodiac chapters, each animal signs off with its lucky numbers for 2025. But what do the numbers represent? In turn, what happens when the lucky number for your sign happens to be an inauspicious (or unlucky) number? This seems a contradiction, but 'context is king'. For example, 5 is typically considered positive due to its association with the five elements (lucky), but the word sounds similar to 'not/without' in Chinese (i.e., unlucky). Also, a combination of numbers can make something perceived to be unlucky become lucky. Using our 5 example once again, when used in conjunction with 4 (i.e., 54), we create a 'without death' combination, which is surely good in the right context!

1	**2**	**3**
Number one symbolises independence and new beginnings. Yet it can be lonely.	Two is a lucky number representing harmony and companionship. It's believed that good things come in pairs.	Three is associated with growth, abundance, and stability.
4	**5**	**6**
The unluckiest number of them all as four sounds like the word for death. Car number plates containing a four are avoided. Some buildings leave out the fourth floor altogether – as often happens with the number thirteen in the west. Ironically, thirteen is unloved in China too as the digits add up to the unfortunate four.	Five is associated with the five Chinese elements – Water, Wood, Fire, Earth, Metal - which together provide perfect balance.	Six is auspicious since it sounds like the word for smooth flowing. Six in your orbit suggests plans will go well for you and obstacles will disappear.
7	**8**	**9**
Seven arouses mixed feelings. It can symbolise energy and growth but also deception. An air of mystery surrounds a seven.	Eight is considered the luckiest number you can have as it's associated with wealth and prosperity. Number plates with the number 8 repeated, the eighth floor of any building, or a house number are highly sought after.	The last single digit number, nine, is the symbol of long life as it's the top of the list.

CHAPTER 2: THE SNAKE

蛇

Snake Years

10 February 1929 – 29 January 1930

27 January 1941 – 14 February 1942

14 February 1953 – 2 February 1954

2 February 1965 – 20 January 1966

18 February 1977 – 6 February 1978

6 February 1989 – 26 January 1990

24 January 2001 – 11 February 2002

10 February 2013 – 30 January 2014

29 January 2025 – 16 February 2026

15 February 2037 – 3 February 2038

Natural Element: Fire

Will 2025 be a Glorious Year for the Snake?

Well, of course, Snake. What a silly question. How could it not be a glorious year when – after more than a decade hibernating away, quietly putting up with all sorts of nonsense from the other ruling signs – you've finally got the chance to come out into the full blaze of the sun and do things properly. Your way!

Fortunately, last year, with your friend the Dragon in charge, things should have gone reasonably well for you, if you were typical of your sign.

The Snake and the Dragon are generally sympathetic towards each other, and you don't like to interfere – (madness to even attempt such a thing with a powerful beast like the Dragon anyway) – but you don't always agree with the way the Dragon goes about proceedings. Totally over the top half the time, as far as the Snake is concerned. So, most Snakes will be emerging into 2025 comfortable in many ways but exhausted. Dragon years tend to be beneficial but tiring for sensitive serpents.

As a result, your first few weeks in the driver's seat might seem deceptively slow, uneventful even. But don't be fooled. 2025 is the year the typical Snake will go into major skin-shedding mode.

All the pent-up restlessness and frustration of previous years is likely to come to the surface, and many Snakes will opt for total transformation. Home, job, car, friends and family even – all are due for (at the very least) an overhaul if not outright replacement.

What makes this upheaval even more doable for the normally restrained Snake is the fact that this is a Wood year, and the Snake's natural element is Fire. Wood supplies Fire with all the energy it needs to burn long and fierce, and since it's your year, Snake, you intend to take full advantage of it.

Many a Snake will be moving house in 2025; very few will be thinking of downsizing. Bigger and better is what the Snake is attracted to now, and why not? You deserve it. That also goes for the Snake car, furnishings, and entire wardrobe. If you can't have what you fancy in your own personal year, when can you?

Career opportunities are likely to fall across the serpent path at this point, too. Typical Snakes are exceptionally intelligent but often overlooked because they tend to be modest and reticent. Yet, with the golden spotlight of the King or Queen of the Year lighting you up like a cinema screen, there's no way your talents won't get noticed and rewarded.

Yet, being the ruler of the year isn't completely like winning the lottery. There is a more serious side. With power comes responsibility. Many a Snake will be expected to help others expand and grow their prospects. Family and friends could be pestering you for favours or even loans. At work, more authority could be put on your shoulders than you'd planned.

Plus, of course, just because you want to transform your entire life, it doesn't mean everyone else will be happy about it. The possible anger beneath the Wood year could suddenly ignite and quite a few Snakes will be forced to calm difficult situations. Fortunately, with all that typical Snake wisdom and charm, this is not difficult… but it is tiring. It's just as well that 2025 is likely to present you with quite a few chances to relax and bask in the sun.

The Wonder of Being a Snake

Come on, admit it. You always knew you were a bit special, didn't you, Snake? Perhaps at some point then, deep down, you were a little dismayed to find your sign was the Snake. How could this be, you might think, when you're such a delightful person? But you probably only feel that way because it's in the West that the Snake gets very bad press.

The very name can be an insult, and people tend to shudder and back away from the real-life creature.

Yet this attitude is to misunderstand the sheer brilliance of this extraordinary beast.

Imagine a creature that has no legs yet can shoot across the ground with lightning speed; a creature that, when peckish, can swallow an animal many times its own size in one gulp; a creature that, when annoyed, can spit venom across a forked tongue; a creature that, for an encore, can slip out of its entire skin to present a brand new, wrinkle-free body beneath.

It sounds so magical; it's difficult to believe such a creature really exists. Yet that's the miracle we call a Snake.

The Chinese have long recognised the exceptional gifts of the Snake and for this reason, in the East, the sign of the Snake is highly respected.

It's associated with wisdom, intelligence, grace, and renewal. The Chinese also believe it's a sign of great beauty, and it's true that most people born under the sign of the Snake have a distinctive poise and attractiveness that draws people to them, even if they're not conventionally beautiful. They are also blessed with a natural grace of movement. They're born dancers with a great appreciation for music.

The Snake is highly intuitive, sometimes psychic too, and perhaps this – along with their mystical link to renewal and rebirth – is the reason for the Snake's long reputation for healing. They instinctively 'know' what ails a person and how to make them feel better, though chances are they couldn't tell you where this knowledge comes from.

Despite all these gifts, the typical Snake is a little reserved. Their restrained manner is often mistaken for shyness. Yet the Snake is not exactly shy, more intensely private. People born under this sign prefer to sit on the sidelines, quietly observing and giving nothing away until they startle everyone with their astute summing up of the situation. They are also excellent readers of character and it's very unwise to lie to a Snake. That penetrating gaze will see straight through falsehoods and should you lose the trust of a Snake, you're unlikely to get it back, ever.

Strangely enough, despite their modest behaviour, the Snake has a reputation for great ambition – due to the creature's determination to swallow prey larger than itself, usually successfully.

For this reason, Snakes have an amazing ability to rise to the top of any career ladder, without apparently making much effort. In fact, at work, some Snakes are even assumed to be chronically lazy because they appear to do as little as possible. What their colleagues fail to realise is that the Snake tires easily and needs to conserve energy as much as possible. While capable of great speed and stamina, the Snake only employs such effort when it's absolutely essential. The rest of the time, Snake works smart rather than hard – but because the Snake is smarter than most, this is usually more than adequate.

The other remarkable thing about people born under this sign is that they'll patiently put up with all manner of unpleasantness and unfavourable situations seemingly forever and then suddenly – snap. They walk away without warning or a backward glance, leaving onlookers stunned.

Only afterwards do people learn that the Snake has been inert and silently brooding for months. But it's no good imploring Snake to return. Snake's actions are swift and irrevocable.

The Snake Home

The Snake home is a special place. Most Snakes need a private sanctuary where they can relax completely and mull over the events of the day, the week, and probably the last ten years. Snakes are great 'mullers' – given to brooding if they don't get out enough.

They also need a tranquil space where they can plot their next move uninterrupted. They're great plotters and planners, too, and prefer to have events thought out in advance.

Those privileged to be invited to the Snake home will find a tasteful, beautifully arranged hideaway with an accent on comfort and clean lines. They may be surprised, too, to discover the quiet Snake is an unexpectedly excellent host. The finest food and drink will be pressed on guests, and visitors will be encouraged to entertain and gossip. Gossip is particularly enjoyed by the Snake. A fun evening is guaranteed – just don't expect to be invited back too often.

Being Friends with the Snake

The Snake makes a loyal and mostly undemanding friend, but they give their friendship sparingly. Intensely private people, it takes a while for them to admit new faces to their inner circle, and even when they do, it's unlikely they will confide all their secrets, ever. Nevertheless, they will support and aid their friends with genuine care. Don't take advantage, though. The Snake tends to see things in black and white. Annoy the Snake (surprisingly easy to do, though you might never know they were upset) or worse, lie to them, and they will cut you off instantly.

Snake Superpowers

Spooky intuition

Can persuade anyone to do anything

Razor-sharp insight

Best Jobs for Snake

Psychiatrist

Beautician

Detective

Acupuncturist

Dancer

Researcher

Counsellor

Perfect Partners

Cupid's arrow can strike anywhere at any time, of course, but once the novelty of new romance wears off, some relationships are easier to maintain than others. Here's a guide to the Snake's compatibility with other signs.

Snake with Snake

This fine-looking couple turn heads wherever they go. Beautiful and perfectly dressed, these two look like the perfect match. They never stop talking and enjoy the same interests, so this could be a successful relationship. Long-term, however, there could be friction. They're both experts at getting what they want using the same sophisticated techniques, so they can see through each other.

Snake with Horse

At some level, perhaps, Horse remembers how Snake beat him in the calendar race, so despite an initial attraction, these two could be wary of each other. Snake is impressed by Horse's energy and athleticism, while Horse admires Snake's elegance and charm. Yet they don't really have much in common. Deep thinking Snake could find Horse rather shallow, and Horse may see Snake as frustratingly enigmatic.

Snake with Goat

Snake and Goat could enjoy many happy hours touring art galleries and exhibitions together. Neither of them craves excitement and harsh, adrenaline-boosting activities, and both appreciate creative artistic personalities. There's no pressure to compete with each other, so these two would sail along quite contentedly. Not a passionate alliance, but they could be happy.

Snake with Monkey

These two clever creatures ought to admire each other if only for their fine minds and, at first, it's possible they might. But unless they're really determined to make it work, it won't be long before active Monkey finds Snake's energy-saving ways irritating, while Snake loses patience with Monkey's endless jokes.

Snake with Rooster

Surprisingly, Snake and Rooster work well together. Both are gorgeous in different ways; they complement each other without competing. Snake's keen eyes can see beneath Rooster's proud facade to the sensitive, unsure person inside, while Rooster appreciates Snake's unobtrusive strength and wise words of encouragement at just the right moment. These two could be inseparable.

Snake with Dog

Some Snakes seem to have an almost hypnotic power and, for some reason, Dog is particularly susceptible to these skills. We've heard of snake charmers, but snakes can be dog charmers and, without even trying, Snakes can find themselves the recipients of Dog devotion. Since the Dog is strong, loyal, and can be fun, Snake is not averse to this but might, in the end, find it boring.

Snake with Pig

Pig and Snake don't have a lot to say to each other. Snake can't be bothered with Pig's endless shopping, and Pig is hurt by Snake's snobbish attitude. They both enjoy the good things in life so a luxury fling could briefly be fun – a shared spa break might be a good idea – but in the long term, this relationship is probably not worth pursuing.

Snake with Rat

The Snake shares Rat's good taste, and being elegant, sophisticated, and smart will delight Rat at first sight. These two get on very well on an intellectual level but perhaps are better as good friends rather than long-term partners. The Snake's love of basking in the sun for hours strikes

Rat as lazy and dull, while Rat's need to rush around doing deals and meeting people seems pointless and wearying to Snake.

Snake with Ox

Like Ox, the Snake is quietly ambitious and not given to racing around unless it's absolutely necessary. Ox, on the other hand, respects Snake's clever brain and understated elegance. These two could quickly discover how beneficial an alliance between them would be. They're both happy to give the other space when required but also step in with support when needed. This could be a very successful match.

Snake with Tiger

Not the best of romances. These two are so fundamentally different that any initial attraction is unlikely to last. Snake likes to bask and soak up the sun, while Tiger wants to explore and discover. Tiger takes in the big picture at a glance and is off to the next challenge, while Snake likes to pause, delve beneath the surface, and consider matters. It wouldn't take long before these two annoy each other.

Snake with Rabbit

This subtle pair could make a good combination. They both understand the value of working behind the scenes, and neither has any desire to wear themselves out on endless adventures. They share a love of art, fine things, and quiet pleasures, and they both enjoy an orderly home. These two could settle down very happily together.

Snake with Dragon

Surprisingly, this couple gets along beautifully. Snake's elegant appearance and quick but subtle mind intrigues Dragon, while Snake admires Dragon's success and endless energy. Snake has no need to battle for the limelight and is quite happy to sit back and support Dragon's schemes from the comfort of a stylish sofa. Which is all the encouragement Dragon needs.

Snake Love 2025 Style

Sizzling is the word when it comes to your love life this year, Snake, and won't you enjoy every minute of it!

True, even in unfavourable years, the sexy Snake has never been short of admirers. There's something about Snake's languid grace, enigmatic smile, and unhurried, fluid way of moving that's almost hypnotic and immensely sensuous.

Once Snake catches someone's eye, that eye is unable to look away, and the rest of the smitten body usually follows. Other signs can only look on with awe and envy. How *do* you do it, Snake?

And that is just Snake's success rate in an average year. Imagine how gorgeous you appear now, Snake, bathed as you are in the enticing glow of Mistress or Master of 2025. Your magic is off the scale, and with all that Wood energy lighting your Fire, you're destined to take full advantage.

Yet, oddly enough, the typical Snake rejects more admirers than they accept. Deep down, you're well aware of your worth, Snake, and you know you can afford to be picky. Only the most appealing prospects will be granted an audience, and they'd better be on their best behaviour.

Single Snakes are spoiled for choice this year, but they could end up being accused of a certain heartlessness. This is because, in 2025 of all years, you're not prepared to compromise. You're not going to settle for 'almost right'. If Mr or Ms Right turns out to be wrong, you're no longer prepared to waste time on retraining them. They're history. You'll slip away with that uncanny knack of yours, and they'll never hear from you again. The Snake perfected ghosting long before it was a thing.

Attached Snakes share the same unyielding mood. Happy partnerships are likely to be blessed and reach new heights of bliss. Loved-up couples could well be creating a new nest, expanding their family or maybe adding a pet or two. But rocky relationships that have been limping along for months could finally hit the buffers this year. The Snake's patience is at an end.

Secrets of Success in 2025

There's no doubt you're on fire this year, Snake. After a slowish start – while you get your bearings and accustom yourself to your new, elevated status – brilliant ideas are suddenly bursting into your mind from every direction.

Moreover, people are taking you even more seriously than they usually do and are likely to agree to whatever you suggest.

The trouble is, you're bound to confuse them all because you're ready to change almost everything, and they don't understand the need for upheaval. There's so much you'd like to do, it's difficult to know where to start and everyone's looking to you for answers. As the decisions and queries pile up, the stress could become overwhelming.

This is where the urge to do your famous skin-shedding routine may kick in – you know, the one where you just walk away without a rearward glance to start anew, leaving complete chaos behind.

Sometimes, when it comes to career, that's not a bad idea if your job is unsatisfying or your business is failing. Many a Snake will say good riddance to their old role this year and strike out in a new direction.

But others are actually better advised to calm down, de-stress, and employ some of that famous Snake wisdom. You can work miracles if you simply hold your nerve, look at the issue from a different angle, and make some creative adjustments. No one's smarter than you, Snake, and this is the year to show the world what you can do.

You have all the ingredients you need for a big success in 2025. Just remember, you're more sensitive than you realise. Stress can de-rail you if you attempt too much at once. So, take things one step at a time, break out that legendary Snake chill, and you'll be amazed at your achievements.

The Snake Year at a Glance

January – After waving 2024 goodbye, what you'd really like is a few duvet days. Go for it, Snake. The rest will do you good.

February – Things are perking up. Slowly, energy is returning. At work, your opinions are welcomed.

March – A whole new look suddenly appeals. New hair, new clothes, new diet. Wow.

April – Someone suggests the gym. It's not usually your thing, but it may be worth trying. New faces at work change the atmosphere. Exciting.

May – Your brilliance is recognised. A promotion or new job beckons.

June – You're asked to organise some sort of group event. Difficult to refuse, and it turns out to be a triumph. You're good at this.

July – A surprise date looks like turning serious. Could a summer of love be on the cards?

August – An exotic overseas trip is too tempting to miss. An intriguing stranger captures your interest.

September – A brilliant idea strikes. You could be starting a whole new business.

October – Past love catches up with you again. They'd like another chance – should you agree? Decisions!

November – You're numero uno at work. You can't put a foot wrong, but you're more interested in moving home.

December – This could be your first Christmas in your new place. If not, you'll be house-hunting the minute Boxing Day's over. Fun times.

Lucky colours for 2025: Red, Black, and Yellow

Lucky numbers for 2025: 2, 8, 9

Three Takeaways

Pace Yourself

Remember, not everyone's as smart as you

Be kind

CHAPTER 3: THE HORSE

Horse Years
30 January 1930 – 16 February 1931
15 February 1942 – 4 February 1943
3 February 1954 – 23 January 1955
21 January 1966 – 8 February 1967
7 February 1978 – 27 January 1979
27 January 1990 – 14 February 1991
12 February 2002 – 31 January 2003
31 January 2014 – 18 February 2015
17 February 2026 – 5 February 2027
4 February 2038 – 23 January 2039
1 February 2041 – 21 January 2042
Natural Element: Fire

Will 2025 be a Glorious Year for the Horse?

Okay, Horse, you're normally one of the bravest and boldest of the zodiac personalities, but even you may be quaking inwardly at the prospect of a Snake-run year. You've been pretty fortunate for quite a while now, you must admit, if you're typical of your sign, because a succession of your besties (plus a few of at least reasonably compatible mates) have been in charge, happy to help you out when the going got tough.

Well, obviously, this pleasant situation was bound to come to an end sometime. So, you now find yourself in 2025, ruled by a creature that tends to make you nervous. The Horse has never been entirely comfortable with the Snake. Possibly, it stems from the days of the race across the river when Snake sneaked over the water wrapped round Horse's leg, then sprang out ahead and beat Horse for sixth place in the zodiac. Deep down, this underhand trick still rankles, and Horse has never trusted Snake since.

Yet the point is, Horse, the Snake doesn't have anything *against* you. In fact, Snake probably finds you very useful at times; after all, you did ferry it across the river even if you didn't mean to. So, there's no need to worry about 2025. You've got a lot going for you this year; you just have to pay a bit more attention to organising your strategy in a more Snake-like way.

For a start, this is a Wood year, which is great news because you're a Fire creature. All that fuel will be charging your energy non-stop. You're the active type at the dullest of times, so in 2025, you'll be fizzing with so much static that you're shooting invisible sparks like a Catherine Wheel.

And that invigorating blaze will last all year, propelling you to achieve more than you ever thought possible – as long as you harness it properly.

The only problem will be deciding what you want to do and where to start. Inspired by the Snake impulse of change, many a Horse will be seized with restlessness.

A move out to the countryside could materialise in 2025 for many Horses as a desire for wide open spaces and the great outdoors takes hold. Where that's not possible, a sudden interest in open-air sports could develop. Who knew you were such a fine athlete, Horse? Marathon running, in particular, could turn out to be a special and very satisfying talent. And don't rule out anything to do with actual, real life horses. You may discover you're a natural when it comes to riding or looking after equines.

For some reason, conventional career matters won't have such an appeal in 2025, though work is ticking over nicely for the typical Horse. Yet, despite this, most Horses won't be short of money. Windfalls, inheritances, or unexpected winnings are set to boost your bank balance in a highly pleasing way, and you'll have no problem deciding how to spend it.

Holidays may take on extra significance this year, too, possibly aided by that cash bonus. Many Horses will suddenly decide to lash out on the trip of a lifetime, or maybe we're talking honeymoons here. Whatever the reason, this holiday is no ordinary break.

And the continuing Wood influence of expansion and growth will be working its magic on the Horse family and social circle in a big way. Expect new faces, new babies, and all manner of exciting additions in every area of life. In fact, most Horses will find themselves rushed off their hooves in the most enjoyable way.

The Wonder of Being a Horse

No need to be modest, Horse; you've always known you were gorgeous.

Even if you're not conventionally good-looking, you're blessed with a strong, healthy physique, thick glossy hair and large, expressive eyes. Always striking, you're admired wherever you go.

In China, the Horse is believed to be a symbol of freedom, and you've only got to see a herd of wild horses galloping joyfully through the countryside to understand why.

People born in the year of the Horse exude a similar magnificence and independence of spirit. Yet they're often misunderstood by other signs. The rest of the zodiac sees that the Horse is a herd animal and also notices that people born under this sign are wonderfully gregarious. Zodiac Horses love to be surrounded by friends, enjoying social occasions or partying, and will grab any chance for a chat. So, the rest of the zodiac puts two and two together and makes twenty-two.

Add to this the Horse's penchant for frequent grooming – they love having their hair brushed, nails beautified, or their feet massaged - and they think they've got you sussed, Horse.

Which is why it can come as a shock when they discover there's a lot more to you than first meets the eye.

For a start, though you love having your gang around you, the typical Horse also requires a lot of 'me time'. The urge to be free is very strong, and when people or situations seem to press too close, the Horse instinct is to race for the hills, metaphorically speaking. One minute, the Horse is there; the next, they've gone and will disappear alone for hours on end, often with no explanation.

The other trait that surprises non-Horses is that despite the wonderful physical strength and courage of the typical Horse, their nerves are very close to the surface. Loud noises, aggressive situations, worrying events, or sudden shocks upset them far more than seems necessary.

Though the brave Horse will attempt to hide the feelings of panic that sweep over them when unfortunate incidents occur, they often come across as moody and difficult as a result.

What's more, the Horse can be a little temperamental. It's mainly because the typical Horse has so much energy and vitality, other signs just can't keep up, and Horse gets impatient. But, also, the typical Horse tends to change its mind quite frequently, which can be annoying for other signs.

And then there's the way Horse can suddenly overreact to an innocent remark that no one else finds offensive. This has more to do with the Horse's love of drama than genuinely hurt feelings. Just occasionally, Horse will throw a moody simply to stir things up and see what happens.

Nobody's perfect, of course, and despite their little foibles, the typical Horse is popular and friendly. They do well at work. As smart and attractive employees, those in authority like having Horse on their staff. The Horse will work hard and charm everyone, yet may not stay around for long. The typical Horse has a habit of starting a job with great enthusiasm but then quickly getting bored. Just when everything seems to be going well, Horse will suddenly up and leave, and pay raises or promises of promotion are unlikely to change the Horse mind. The lure of pastures new is just too strong to resist.

The Horse Home

The thing about the Horse home is that Horse isn't often in it. Home is where Horse keeps its 'stuff' and also goes to sleep or unwind.

The rest of the time, the Horse likes to be out. Horse loves to entertain – and the more friends or family, the merrier – but reckons the nearest pub or restaurant makes the ideal setting for the get-together.

Visitors are most likely to enter the Horse home just briefly, when picking Horse up en-route to the next adventure. They are likely to trip over the odd dog or two, various discarded trainers, or items of sports equipment. Further inside, the furnishings tend to be comfortable and well-worn, enlivened by various practical gadgets in the kitchen and living room, and shelves groaning with grooming aids in the bathroom.

In fact, the typical Horse home is functional, catering perfectly to Horse's needs and bare of unnecessary fripperies like scatter cushions and pot plants. Just the way Horse likes it, in fact.

Being Friends with the Horse

It's not difficult to strike up a friendship with the typical Horse. Horse is usually friendly, charming, and ready to be sociable. Just don't expect to be an exclusive bestie – Horse has nothing against besties but can't see the point of confining itself to just one or two. The Horse prefers to recruit an ever-changing number of special mates.

Despite this, the Horse is good company as long as you can keep up. The typical equine bores easily and needs constant changes of scenery, preferably with some physical activity thrown in.

Horse will want to round up the gang to go rock-climbing, jogging, or maybe paintballing, attend sports events or camp out at the latest festival. And if there's a competitive element involved, so much the better. Life with Horse is never dull.

Yet, be prepared for the jovial Horse to suddenly take offence at some tiny remark and stomp off in a huff. The tantrum doesn't last long and Horse usually returns later as if nothing happened. The truth is Horse feelings are not as robust as Horse pretends, and can be bruised easily by the most inadvertent and unintentional comment.

Horse Superpowers

Vibrant energy

Infectious enthusiasm

Youthful charm

Best Jobs for Horse

Athlete

Personal Trainer

Car Salesman

Tour Guide

Gym Coach

Hair Stylist

Perfect Partners

Cupid's arrow can strike anywhere at any time, of course, but once the novelty of new romance wears off, some relationships are easier to maintain than others. Here's a guide to the Horse's compatibility with other signs.

Horse with Horse

No doubt about it, these two make a magnificent couple, and any foals in the family would be spectacular. They certainly understand each other, particularly their shared need for both company and alone time, so in general, they get on well. The only tricky part could come if they both grew anxious over the same issue at the same time. Neither would find it easy to calm the other.

Horse with Goat

Goat and Horse just click! These two love kicking up their heels and trotting off into the green. Goat doesn't need to go far or do anything strenuous but is always up for a break in routine, while Horse doesn't do routine at all, so is constantly on the lookout for a partner ready to escape. This couple rarely considers the consequences but, mostly, they don't need to.

Horse with Monkey

Uh oh – best not attempted unless it's love at first sight. Monkey and Horse have wildly different outlooks and can't seem to see eye to eye on anything. They're both lively but in different ways that don't complement each other. Monkey will consider Horse's moods illogical and pointless, while Horse is irritated that Monkey makes no attempt to understand how Horse feels. Very hard work.

Horse with Rooster

The eye-catching Rooster intrigues Horse while Rooster appreciates Horse's strength and agility. They can enjoy many stimulating dates together. Yet, in the long run, this couple may not be able to provide the stability the other needs. They're both sensitive types but in different ways. After a while, the relationship could run out of steam.

Horse with Dog

Both good friends of man, these two can make a formidable team. Dog understands the occasional need for solitude while admiring Horse's strength and agility. Horse, meanwhile, senses Dog's loyalty and down-to-earth nature. Both lovers of the great outdoors and physical activity, they'll never be short of adventures to share. A promising long-term relationship.

Horse with Pig

Pig and Horse are good companions. Horse is soothed by easy-going Pig, and Pig is proud to be seen with such an alluring creature as Horse. They don't have a lot of interests in common, but they don't antagonise each other either. They can jog along amicably for quite a while, but in the long term, they may find they each want more than the other can provide.

Horse with Rat

Rat and Horse both fizz with energy, and they love action and looking good, yet this is not seen as an ideal partnership. Nothing's impossible, of course, but these two will have to work hard to find harmony. The Rat will admire Horse's enthusiasm and cheerful approach but become impatient to discover Horse can also be fiery and emotional. Horse, on the other hand, can find Rat's risk-taking behaviour extremely worrying.

Horse with Ox

Long ago on many Western farms, Ox was replaced by the Horse, and it may be that Ox has never forgotten and never forgiven. At any rate, these two – despite both being big, strong animals – are not usually friends. Horse is too flighty and frivolous to interest Ox for long, while Ox's methodical, careful ways will irritate the Horse. Best not to go there.

Horse with Tiger

This athletic pair gets on pretty well. They both like physical pursuits, testing their strength out of doors or just enjoying the feel of the wind in their hair and the ground under their feet. True, Horse may not quite understand Tiger's plans for world domination, but it doesn't really matter. Horse is happy to be loyal to such a charismatic partner. As they're both moody, there could be rows, but making up is exciting.

Horse with Rabbit

This could be tricky. It's fairly unlikely that Horse and Rabbit would ever end up on a date, but if they did and there was a strong attraction, it could lead to a love/hate relationship. Rabbit's neat and tidy ways would enrage Horse, and Horse's unpredictable moods and over-the-top reactions would annoy Rabbit. Soon, Horse is likely to bolt for the hills or Rabbit retreat to its burrow.

Horse with Dragon

The athletic Horse is pretty good at keeping up with the dashing Dragon. And Dragon appreciates a partner who enjoys getting out and about as much as Dragon does. Yet Horse might grow weary of Dragon's constant new projects and resent having to be involved. Horse likes to go off and do Horsey things at frequent intervals, which Dragon tends to view as disloyal. This relationship could get fiery.

Horse with Snake

At some level, perhaps Horse remembers how Snake beat him in the calendar race, so despite an initial attraction, these two could be wary of each other. Snake is impressed by Horse's energy and athleticism, while Horse admires Snake's elegance and charm. Yet they don't really have much in common. Deep thinking Snake could find Horse rather shallow, and Horse may see Snake as frustratingly enigmatic.

Horse Love 2025 Style

Brace yourself, Horse. Love is where it's at for you this year. Where last year you were preoccupied with sorting out your career, if you were typical of your sign, and didn't have much time for romance, the good news is that in 2025, it's just the opposite.

Career matters are no longer so interesting or maybe just not so demanding. Whatever the difference, you're bored with all that dull, serious stuff, and now you're in the mood to play. And since you're such a head-turner, you won't be short of playmates.

What's more, with time on your hands to explore new products and styles, you're at your burnished best right now, exuding a movie star vibe wherever you go. Prospective partners are falling over themselves to make your acquaintance.

Yet, for once, you're not so interested in playing the field, Horse. You're looking for love with a capital 'L', and it seems that – this year – you might very well find it. Many a Horse could be planning a wedding before the year's out.

Attached Horses can look forward to a summer of love as long as the relationship survived the work-related absences of 2024. Now, the Horse fires are blazing strongly, and the two of you are together in the same place at last, to make the most of things.

Secrets of Success in 2025

While it's difficult to get your mind off romance this year, Horse, you're quite capable of enjoying success in 2025.

Although the Snake isn't your fondest cheerleader, it's a fair judge and will come to your aid if you just adopt a more Snake-like attitude to work. Unlikely as it seems, you're both Fire creatures after all and at some deep level, you share a basic understanding – so you ought to be able to get along professionally.

The thing that irritates the Snake, Horse, is the way you tend to gallop off after a venture that captures your attention without doing enough investigation and research. This haste inevitably leads to disappointment, and you end up losing valuable time and money on failed projects.

Then there's the way your love of novelty (and tendency to be impatient) means you often give up on a plan long before it's had time to come to fruition, simply because it's grown tedious.

These habits annoy the Snake, Horse, and good fortune will elude you while you indulge them. Yet, if you'll just curb your enthusiasm when a new offer appears, and do your due diligence (plus, if all looks promising, you stick to the plan through the inevitable ups and downs), you could literally transform your world.

With a little discipline, 2025 could be your most successful year ever, Horse, and set you up for decades to come.

The Horse Year at a Glance

January – Uh oh. You're feeling nervous. Keep calm; things will work out fine.

February – Out of the blue, a new job offer comes your way. It looks exciting, but is it time for a change?

March – You get along with most, but now an awkward person enters your circle. Don't overreact.

April – An exciting romance is brewing. Is a spring break on the cards?

May – Stern faces at work bring you down a bit. You can turn things around.

June – Phew. You're back on course, and a cash windfall comes your way.

July – The sun's shining, and you're off to play. A family celebration beckons.

August – New love hots up, but jealousy is in the air. Are you too popular, Horse?

September – A friend in need asks for help. You haven't much time, but do your best.

October – Reunions all around. Old school mates, old lovers get in touch. Lively gatherings brighten the month.

November – A shopping spree beckons. You've got more people to buy for, and it's not long til Christmas.

December – a romantic Christmas is in store. You could be whisked away for some festive fun.

Lucky colours for 2025: Yellow, Pink, Purple

Lucky numbers for 2025: 2, 3, 7

Three Takeaways

Think long haul
Don't give up
Refuse to take things personally

CHAPTER 4: THE GOAT

Goat Years

17 February 1931 – 5 February 1932

5 February 1943 – 24 January 1944

24 January 1955 – 11 February 1956

9 February 1967 – 29 January 1968

28 January 1979 – 15 February 1980

15 February 1991 – 3 February 1992

1 February 2003 – 21 January 2004

19 February 2015 – 7 February 2016

6 February 2027 – 25 January 2028

24 January 2039 – 11 February 2040

Natural Element: Fire

Will 2025 be a Glorious Year for the Goat?

Phew, after the rollercoaster that was 2024, you're probably looking forward to kicking off your shoes, pulling on your favourite jim-jams, and hiding away somewhere snug and quiet for the next few months to get over it, Goat.

Well, the good news is Snake quite agrees with you. 2025 is set to be much more favourable to Goat sensitivities.

It's not that 2024 was bad for the typical Goat. Quite the reverse for many people born under this sign. When you get your breath back, you'll probably notice that you've come a long way, made a great deal of progress, and the past year contained a lot of good things. It's just there was too MUCH, of everything, and it was all too fast for the reflective Goat.

Happily, the Snake is much more on your wavelength, Goat. While 2025 is another Wood year – bringing with it the same urge for growth and expansion – the Snake ensures that the pace is toned down. Snake doesn't like to be rushed, and neither do you, Goat.

Change is still nagging insistently at the Goat door, but it's much more manageable this year. It looks as if many a Goat will be moving home in 2025, but not in a forced, panicky way. It's not essential you move, Goat, just that the idea of down-sizing, up-sizing, or simply having a change of scene suddenly seems appealing. You can afford to take your time and enjoy checking out a few contenders in a leisurely fashion, but if nothing takes your fancy, you can just stay put.

Ironically, when you don't really mind whether you find the perfect place or not, you're more likely to stumble upon your dream home. Might as well start packing now, Goat.

The same goes for that job or business. Polite, happy-go-lucky Goat can make the best of most work situations, but that doesn't mean they're the ideal fit. So, this year, the typical Goat is inspired to look around for something better (very discreetly, of course). And chances are you'll find it, Goat.

The great thing about this Wood year for you, Goat, is that – like the Snake – the Goat is a Fire creature. True, Wood is a little nervous around Fire, for obvious reasons, so opportunities and good fortune may be a little hesitant in arriving, but arrive they will. In the meantime, all the fuel the Wood element provides will give you energy to burn. You'll certainly have the stamina to finish whatever you start.

Artistic Goats that launched creative projects last year are particularly fortunate in 2025, and will see demand for their work rocket. Musical Goats will be deluged with requests for performances, lessons, or just the pleasure of their talented company.

And if you missed out on beginning something new last year, Goat, 2025 will provide you with a second chance. Now is the time to acquire a new skill, experiment with a new hobby, or dabble in a different craft. Something you learn in the next few months could prove very lucrative for you in years to come.

Few Goats will end up being short of cash this year. The typical Goat isn't particularly interested in wealth, in any case, but the friendly Snake will ensure there's always enough to do what you want.

And finally, many signs are seeing their families expand this year and the Goat is no exception. You can look forward to countless joyful get-togethers in 2025, Goat, that will fill you with happiness.

The Wonder of Being a Goat

You've always been the modest type, Goat, that's obvious but you really have to accept you're unique. There's no one quite like you, and that's just a fact. What's more, even though you never push yourself forward, if you're typical of your sign, other signs seem to know this instinctively. Goats are usually treated with respect wherever they go, despite their unassuming manner.

The Goat modesty is puzzling at first since the live animal is famously sure-footed. And, in fact, despite their diffident appearance, the typical zodiac Goat rarely puts a foot wrong. Maybe their apparent lack of confidence is down to a certain confusion over their identity in the world. To this day, some authorities know the sign as the Sheep. Others, in more macho style, have it down as the Ram. But, either way, there's a certain ambiguity about Goat's energy.

The confusion seems to stem from different translations of the original Chinese word back in the mists of time. But what's in a name, after all? The important point is that whether you're called Goat, Sheep, or Ram, we're talking about a sign that symbolises the beautiful qualities of peace and harmony. Not only that, it's the eighth sign of the zodiac, and according to Chinese lore, the number eight is believed to be a lucky number and associated with growth and prosperity.

So, the Goat has every reason to be proud. And it turns out that although this gentle sign would rather avoid conflict wherever possible, it's not the pushover more aggressive types might assume.

Back the Goat into a corner, and bullies will be amazed at the feisty response. This is a Fire creature, after all, and when pushed too far, the Goat temper can suddenly burst into flames. Too late, the bully may remember that real live Goats have sharp horns for a reason and know how to use them.

Most of the time, of course, people born in a Goat year are known as the sweetest and friendliest of signs. They are tolerant and kind, have no wish to be competitive, and want to see the best in everyone they meet.

They are so agreeable in fact, no one notices that the Goat usually ends up doing exactly what it pleases. Deep down, the Goat is quietly stubborn, and once it's made up its mind, it rarely changes it. The great thing about the Goat, though, is that it has no wish to force others to agree. It will happily go it alone with whatever course of action it decides upon. You can join Goat or abstain as you wish; the Goat is perfectly content either way but nothing will deter it from its chosen path.

Yet despite their laid-back exterior, few Goats are as calm as they appear. Conflict, harsh words, and stressful situations upset them deeply, and they will worry silently for weeks until all is resolved.

The typical Goat adores lovely things and sees beauty all around in the most unlikely of objects. They're not naturally materialistic and view money merely as a useful tool to create the lifestyle they prefer. And we're not talking vast mansions, designer clothes, or fancy cars here.

An attractive home, a pretty garden, and a characterful run-around to get them where they want to go if they're too far from a bus route will suit the typical Goat just fine, as long as they've also got time to enjoy the things they enjoy.

Most Goats are born artistic. Many have some wonderful talent that takes them far, but even the Goats who can't paint, sculpt, design or write songs tend to have an eye for colour and proportion and an ever-changing list of crafts they're dying to try. The true Goat is rarely bored.

The Goat home

The typical Goat home tends to captivate visitors. They're charmed and surprised because – whether it's a tiny flat, modest cottage, or spacious villa – it somehow manages to exude a quirky vibe that's both homely and stylish at the same time.

Goat pays no attention to fashion and is not interested in status symbols or trying to impress. Yet, the Goat's natural artistic flair ensures that no matter how they throw unlikely objects together, everything settles miraculously and in perfect harmony.

Every Goat home is unique because the typical Goat has little interest in chain stores and mass-produced furnishings. Instead, Goat prefers to potter from junk shop to car boot sale, from charity outlet to auction house, gathering unusual treasures as they go. Goat has even been known to rescue unloved items from abandoned skips. And, of course, each precious find has to be allocated a new berth, chez Goat. Too big, too small? No problem. Goat is the master or mistress of upcycling and reworking.

The resulting collection of mismatched and reimagined objects shouldn't work, but thanks to Goat's talents, it does. Eclectic is the word for the typical Goat home decor style. Many visitors have tried to recreate the effect, but none succeed. That's the genius of the Goat.

Being Friends with the Goat

It's not difficult being friends with the Goat. Amiable and easy-going, the Goat gets on with almost everyone. Few ever fall out with the equable Goat. In fact, the Goat is so unsettled by cross words and conflict it will frequently wear itself out acting as peacemaker between warring parties.

The Goat is also highly undemanding. Should you wish to accompany Goat on some Goaty expedition – most likely to some art sale or restoration yard – Goat is delighted to have your company. But if it's not your thing, Goat totally understands and will happily go alone.

The only potential problem is that Goat expects friends to be equally undemanding. If your chosen entertainment is not appealing to Goat, Goat sees nothing amiss in saying 'no thank you'. So, should you require a friend who will drop everything to keep you company, Goat is possibly not the best choice. Clingy, needy types are too stressful for the Goat constitution.

Then again, the Goat can often turn stubborn over some apparently small, insignificant detail and refuse to budge, even when their position seems unreasonable and not in their best interests. No point trying to talk them around. You just have to accept their point of view and move on.

Goat Superpowers

Tenacity

Creativity

Self-Reliance

Best Jobs for Goat

Potter

Gardener

Antique Dealer

Interior Designer

Reflexologist

Charity Worker

Perfect Partners

Cupid's arrow can strike anywhere at any time, of course, but once the novelty of new romance wears off, some relationships are easier to maintain than others. Here's a guide to the Goat's compatibility with other signs.

Goat with Goat

When things are going well, you won't find a happier couple than two Goats. They are perfectly in tune with each other's creative natures and understand when to do things together and when to step back and give the other space. And since they both share the same interests, their together times are always fun. Yet, when practical problems arise, neither can easily cope. With a helpful friend on speed dial, this would work.

Goat with Monkey

Monkey and Goat are different, but in a good way. Though they don't quite 'get' each other deep down, Goat admires Monkey's lively personality and magical ability to come up with solutions for everything, while curious Monkey enjoys Goat's knowledge of the arts and the unusual. Long-term, Goat might not present enough of a challenge for Monkey but, with effort, it's a promising match.

Goat with Rooster

Peaceful Goat is not one to make feathers fly, so these two are unlikely to fall out, but they're unlikely to find perfect compatibility, either. Goat is unable to give Rooster the regular ego boosts that make Rooster thrive, while Rooster is baffled by Goat's unpredictable devotion to impractical projects or people. Misunderstandings are likely.

Goat with Dog

This is another relationship that could be tricky. Loyal Dog would be quite willing to stand by Goat when practical problems loom but could end up irritated by Goat's inability to learn from previous mistakes and so keeps making them. Goat can't understand why Dog gets so bothered. With care, these two could learn to live together.

Goat with Pig

Happy-go-lucky Pig and laid-back Goat make a good pair. They hate to stir up trouble and always look for a peaceful solution to any challenge. Ideally, they'd avoid the challenge altogether. They could be very contented together as long as Pig's spending and Goat's inability to deal with finances doesn't get them into trouble.

Goat with Rat

The Rat is charmed by carefree Goat and fascinated by its artistic talent and happy knack of living in the present. Easy-going Goat tends to like everyone, so is perfectly content to enjoy Rat's company. These two can get along fine, yet they don't really understand each other deep down. Long-term, the Rat may find Goat's lack of interest in the practical side of life irritating.

Goat with Ox

Though these two share artistic natures (even if in the case of the Ox, they're well hidden), deep down they don't 'get' one another. Ox may be beguiled at first by Goat's friendly, easy-going manner but then disappointed to discover Goat seems to find everyone equally delightful, even those who are plainly unworthy. Goat, on the other hand, can't understand why Ox won't lighten up more. This relationship would require a lot of effort and compromise.

Goat with Tiger

Tiger and Goat don't have a lot in common. While their aims and temperaments are quite different, they are both sociable creatures, and Goat wouldn't mind Tiger attracting all the attention when they're out together. Tiger, in return, would appreciate Goat's lack of jealousy and generosity of spirit. Yet, in the long-term, they're likely to drift apart as they follow their different interests.

Goat with Rabbit

Wow! One glance across a crowded room, and that's it for Goat and Rabbit. Rabbit instantly recognises and appreciates Goat's innate style and authenticity, while Goat admires Rabbit's restrained elegance and understated intellect. Both are quiet, home-loving types; they also adore exploring and acquiring fine things. This couple will never be bored.

Goat with Dragon

Goat tends to baffle the busy Dragon. Dragon can see Goat is the creative type but can't understand why Goat doesn't appear to be working very hard when so much could be achieved. In fact, if they stayed together long enough, Dragon could help Goat make the most of many talents, but it's unlikely either of them can sustain enough interest for this to happen.

Goat with Snake

Snake and Goat could enjoy many happy hours touring art galleries and exhibitions together. Neither of them craves excitement and harsh, adrenaline-boosting activities, and both appreciate creative, artistic personalities. There's no pressure to compete with each other, so these two would sail along quite contentedly. Not a passionate alliance, but they could be happy.

Goat with Horse

Goat and Horse just click! These two love kicking up their heels and trotting off into the green. Goat doesn't need to go far or do anything strenuous but is always up for a break in routine, while Horse doesn't do routine at all, so is constantly on the lookout for a partner ready to escape. This couple rarely considers the consequences, but mostly, they don't need to.

Goat Love 2025 Style

Let the good times roll, Goat. You're set to have fun this year. Now the pressures of 2024 are receding into the background, you can relax and concentrate on enjoying yourself.

And it's not going to be difficult to find plenty of playmates to keep you company, Goat. For a start, you get on with almost everyone, and then secondly (although you don't realise it), your unusual but striking style always catches the eye and is highly alluring.

You don't set out to turn heads, Goat, but you just can't help it. Your authenticity and sincerity shine out, and other signs are drawn to you. Then, when they notice the way you don't judge but accept everyone as they are, they tend to become completely smitten.

The typical Goat tends not to notice this at first, and when they do, it can become problematic if Goat doesn't reciprocate the feelings. Disentangling yourself from unwanted loves could become stressful this year, Goat, so try not to give mixed messages.

Nevertheless, this is another Wood year, and you're a Fire creature, Goat, with fewer responsibilities than before. You're so hot right now you'd be crazy not to enjoy a few blazes.

Attached Goats are likely to inspire a rekindling of their relationship. With stress levels reducing, you and your partner are ready to frolic. You're in the mood for romantic weekends away, cosy evenings around the fire, and long lie-ins in the morning. Enjoy.

Secrets of Success in 2025

The typical Goat likes to quibble about the concept of success. What does it even mean anyway? Is it measured purely in terms of figures on a spreadsheet, piles of cash in the bank, or is it a happy home life and countless friends?

Goat would probably opt for the latter. Yet you don't need to make a choice, Goat. It's possible to have more of it all if you organise yourself better.

Fortunately, the Snake – while being one of the smartest operators on the planet – is far more sympathetic to the Goat's way of working than last year's impatient Dragon.

The Snake understands that Goats will work tirelessly – 24/7 – on a project that inspires them, scarcely pausing even to eat. Yet Goats can barely bring themselves to get out of bed for tasks that are mundane and dull.

So, Snake figures, simply apply that old saying: 'Find a job you love, and you'll never have to work a day in your life again' and you'll be fine.

If you haven't already found your calling, Goat, this year Snake will help. All you need to do is get out there and start searching. When you find it, you'll just know, and everything will fall into place. You won't look back.

Time is on your side in the hunt, Goat, except for one thing. If you're typical of your sign, you're not very good with bills. No one likes them, of course, but the Goat finds them so unpleasant it prefers not to think of them at all. Which inevitably leads to forgotten payments, final demands, and the risk of serious consequences. Refuse to procrastinate, Goat. Just sort them immediately, and 2025 will be wonderful.

The Goat Year at a Glance

January – The festivities are over, but things are still busy at Goat's. Pace yourself.

February – The workplace has lost its sparkle. Maybe you can brighten it up, Goat. Spread some cheer.

March – Excitement all around. Looks like you've found some sort of treasure, Goat. A new job, new home, or simply a huge bargain – it's good news.

April – A well-meaning friend is trying to advise you, Goat. It wouldn't hurt to listen.

May – A spring break with a bestie tempts you. Why not go for it?

June – Love is in the air. A new face in your circle catches your eye. This could go places.

July – Uh oh, romance is brewing nicely, but there's jealousy in the background. Try to calm things.

August – A smooth talker has a get-rich-quick scheme. Sounds promising, but you're no expert. Talk to a professional.

September – A misunderstanding at work causes problems. Try not to stress. Investigate instead.

October – Someone tries to push you around. They're polite and reasonable, but you won't stand for it. Quite right, Goat.

November – You're considering a crafty Christmas. Is there time to hand-make personal gifts all around? Are you sure, Goat?

December – Fabulous festivities split between your place and the families. The gifts work out well, wherever they came from.

Lucky colours for 2025: Jade, Crimson, Chestnut

Lucky numbers for 2025: 2, 7

Three Takeaways

Go a little crazy – experiment

Create a private sanctuary

Have confidence – your gifts are unique

CHAPTER 5: THE MONKEY

Monkey Years

6 February 1932 – 25 January 1933

25 January 1944 – 12 February 1945

12 February 1956 – 30 January 1957

30 January 1968 – 16 February 1969

16 February 1980 – 4 February 1981

4 February 1992 – 22 January 1993

22 January 2004 – 8 February 2005

8 February 2016 – 27 January 2017

26 January 2028 – 12 February 2029

12 February 2040 – 31 January 2041

Natural Element: Metal

Will 2025 be a Glorious Year for the Monkey?

Okay, Monkey. Would you like the good news or the not-so-good news? Well, the not-so-good news isn't bad. It's just that last year, you were flavour of the whole 12 months, thanks to your great friendship with the ruler of 2024, the Dragon. Obviously, you can't be the most favoured sign every year and – in 2025 – you're not. Those special privileges the typical Monkey enjoyed last year are not on offer now.

It's not that you and the Snake loathe each other. Just that the Snake is no fonder of you, Monkey, than of a lot of other signs, so will not single you out for extra favours as the Dragon did.

And the good news? Well, the good news is it doesn't matter a bit, Monkey! Your sign is so clever and adaptable it doesn't need preferential treatment to do well. In fact, after a while, you tend to get bored when things are flowing along too smoothly, if you're typical of your sign.

That brilliant brain of yours needs puzzles to solve, difficulties to overcome, rules to evade, authorities to annoy. When all doors swing open automatically, and everyone says 'yes' to even your most outrageous suggestions, you're not really happy, Monkey. You need a challenge to feel satisfied.

So, the chances are you could end up enjoying 2025 even more than 2024 because there'll be plenty of situations to pit your wits against.

The one thing that won't be too much of a worry is finance. The Wood energy of the year is helping your cash to grow, and in any case, money loves Metal signs to which the Monkey happens to belong. Pay rises, unexpected wins, rebates, or even discovering an item you want to sell is worth a whole lot more than you expected – any or all could increase your bank balance this year. Just don't allow Snake's Fire to tempt you to burn through it too fast.

Issues are more likely to come in the form of disagreements with colleagues and loved ones or even authority figures. Why is everyone turning so awkward all of a sudden, Monkey? Surely it can't be you?

This strange phenomenon could have something to do with many a Monkey's sudden desire to do a Snake and cast off their old life for something new. Partners and workmates may not be too happy about the Monkey's previously unmentioned need for completely fresh pastures.

You could well end the year in a completely different home, in a completely different county, and with a completely different job, Monkey. It won't be easy, but you love a tussle.

The more opposition you encounter, the more you enjoy devising complicated routes and strategies to get around the blocks. And when you succeed – which, of course, you will - you'll feel hugely pleased with yourself.

Just step carefully around those authority types. Some Monkeys could find themselves accidentally embroiled in legal battles – and it could take all that simian ingenuity to extract yourself.

The Wonder of Being a Monkey

Wonder is the right word, Monkey. People born under this intriguing sign really are wonders in their own right. In China, the Monkey is associated with justice, intelligence, and sometimes a certain cunning, while in the West, they're also associated with great agility, curiosity, and a mischievous spirit.

Well, basically, zodiac Monkey, that's you. Deep down, you embody all these qualities in varying degrees. Take agility. You may not be a born gymnast, but if you put your mind to it and you're typical of your sign, you find you have a natural flexibility combined with a raw energy that enables you to master any number of physical activities that take your fancy.

The only thing stopping you is a lack of interest. Yet onlookers can tell, simply by the speed of your movements and the dexterity with which you manipulate any item you happen to be using, you're exceptionally deft and nimble.

Then, there's your enquiring mind. The Monkey child is the one that prises open its phone case to see what's inside, empties the contents of the food cupboard into mum's biggest bowl to see how the resulting mixture comes out, and collects snails in the garden to set up a gastropod race.

Adult Monkeys are highly intelligent, but not necessarily in an academic way. They enjoy puzzles, quizzes, and tricky tasks such as assembling intricate flat-pack furniture. They excel at problem-solving of every kind. They also have a strong sense of humour and a weakness for practical jokes that may not appeal to other signs.

Basically, the Monkey needs constant mental stimulation, and when this is in short supply, Monkey's mischievous streak tends to get activated. The resulting mayhem is not usually malicious, simply a way of keeping Monkey entertained, yet these antics often get Monkey into trouble. More awkward still, the Monkey has an instinctive distrust of authority and delights in bending the rules and provoking those in charge. Protesting when caught, it was only a joke, doesn't usually help.

Yet beneath the exterior clown, the Monkey is a great survivor. Most Monkeys know they can afford to play around because they have brainpower to spare. The constant fun and games mask an astute mind with an aptitude for handling money. The Monkey will always do well while apparently not even trying.

The Monkey Home

The phrase most often heard in describing the Monkey home is: 'It'll be nice when it's finished.' The Monkey home is in a constant state of renovation. It's usually a stop-start affair because Monkey tends to begin alterations in a fit of enthusiasm, gets bored, and then takes a break, during which it sees an even better design and resolves to scrap the previous idea to start all over again.

Yet beneath the dust sheets and paint cans, Monkey is likely to have all the latest gadgets and mechanical aids. Anything that can be operated from the Monkey phone, preferably from another continent, will be incorporated whether Monkey needs it or not.

And Monkey is also likely to aspire to a home gym, games room, and maybe even a cinema, should funds permit. Yet, despite all the planned comforts, the typical Monkey often ends up entertaining elsewhere. They just can't abide all that tedious planning and shopping and – in any case – they love a change of scene.

Being Friends with the Monkey

It requires quite a bit of energy and a good sense of humour to be friends with a Monkey. But if you can stand the pace, it's a rewarding relationship. Being around Monkey tends to be a laugh-a-minute affair.

The primate, when in a good mood, loves to entertain and will delight whatever company is around with witty conversation, zany jokes, and crazy ideas. They like to be the centre of attention, too, so if you're not the competitive type and are quite happy to remain the audience, they will appreciate you even more.

They're also active, restless, and can't cope with the same old, same old. They love to explore new haunts, novel entertainments, and exotic foods.

These lively souls need a broad minded, intelligent companion, and you have to be prepared for the odd practical joke which you may not find too funny.

And it's not an entirely undemanding friendship. Monkey can forgive many things but will not stand for being bored. Should the Monkey find you tedious, they'll just melt away.

Monkey Superpowers

Quick wit

Dexterity

Financial wizardry

Best Jobs 2025

Scientist

Acrobat

Inventor

Politician

Comedian

Retail Worker

Perfect Partners

Cupid's arrow can strike anywhere at any time, of course, but once the novelty of new romance wears off, some relationships are easier to maintain than others. Here's a guide to the Monkey compatibility with other signs.

Monkey with Monkey

It's not always the case that opposites attract. More often, like attracts like, and when two Monkeys get together, they find each other delightful. At last, they've met another brain as quick and agile as their own and a person who relishes practical jokes as much as they do. What's more, this is a partner that shares a constant need for change and novelty. Yet, despite this, two Monkeys can often end up competing with each other. As long as they can recognise this, and laugh about it, they'll be fine.

Monkey with Rooster

While not a perfect match, these two have got a lot of time for each other. Monkey recognises the intelligent brain beneath Rooster's plumage, while Rooster admires Monkey's ability to entertain a crowd, and they both adore socialising. They could enjoy many fun dates together. Long-term, though, Rooster may tire of Monkey's jokes.

Monkey with Dog

Monkey finds Dog intriguing. Monkey senses Dog's strength of character coupled with its playful streak, which fits well with Monkey's love of games. Dog, meanwhile, appreciates Monkey's energy and light-hearted approach. Yet, before long, Monkey's disdain for rules will grate on Dog's instinctive love of them. They cannot agree in this area, and it could lead to arguments.

Monkey with Pig

On the surface, these two might seem an unlikely couple. Yet Pig enjoys Monkey's fun and humour while Monkey is happy to be admired uncritically. What's more, Monkey's inventive mind can solve any difficulties caused by Pig's spending, and since Monkey can't resist a challenge, the opportunity to retrain Pig, or at least find a way to obtain purchases cheaper, could help the relationship last.

Monkey with Rat

Unlikely as it might appear, mischievous Monkey and the clever Rat make a good partnership. Their quick minds, sociable natures, and love of novelty ensure that they're never bored together. True, Rat might sometimes feel that Monkey is too inclined to skim over the surface of things and could do with being more serious at times, but Monkey's ingenuity and audaciousness always saves the day. Both can have a weakness for gambling, though, so need to take care.

Monkey with Ox

The naughty Monkey scandalises Ox but in such an amusing way that Ox can't help laughing. Monkey, on the other hand, is equally amused to find an audience that is so easy to shock. This unlikely pair enjoy each other's company and get on surprisingly well. Yet, right from the start, it's probably obvious to both that a long-term relationship couldn't last. A fun flirtation, though, could be a terrific tonic for them both.

Monkey with Tiger

Tiger can't help being intrigued by sparkling Monkey, and Monkey is flattered by such interest. Who wouldn't enjoy being admired by such a fabulous creature? But irrepressible Monkey just can't help teasing, and being teased is not a sensation Tiger is familiar with (or appreciates). Unless the attraction is very strong, these two will wind each other up until they can bear it no longer and part.

Monkey with Rabbit

Mercurial Monkey doesn't really 'get' Rabbit. The Monkey can appreciate how well Rabbit operates and sees this approach gets good results, but it's all too picky and slow for Monkey. Rabbit, on the other hand, is amused by Monkey's quick wit and clever ways but deplores Monkey's slapdash, sometimes devious tactics. Very unlikely to work out.

Monkey with Dragon

These two are likely to hit it off immediately. Each is attracted to the other's intelligence and lively presence, and Dragon's exuberance doesn't overwhelm hyperactive Monkey. What's more, although they both enjoy being surrounded by a crowd, Monkey only wants to make people laugh, while Dragon hopes to inspire them to a cause. There is no conflict, so this couple can help each other to go far.

Monkey with Snake

These two clever creatures ought to admire each other if only for their fine minds, and at first, it's possible they might. But unless they're really determined to make it work, it won't be long before active Monkey finds Snake's energy-saving ways irritating, while Snake loses patience with Monkey's endless jokes.

Monkey with Horse

Uh oh – best not attempted unless it's love at first sight. Monkey and Horse have wildly different outlooks and can't seem to see eye to eye on anything. They're both lively but in different ways that don't complement each other. Monkey will consider Horse's moods illogical and pointless, while Horse is irritated that Monkey makes no attempt to understand how Horse feels. Very hard work.

Monkey with Goat

Monkey and Goat are different, but in a good way. Though they don't quite 'get' each other deep down, Goat admires Monkey's lively personality and magical ability to come up with solutions for everything, while curious Monkey enjoys Goat's knowledge of the arts and the unusual. Long-term, Goat might not present enough of a challenge for Monkey, but with effort, it's a promising match.

Monkey Love 2025 Style

To be honest, Monkey, where you are concerned, every year is a good year for love if you want it to be. Even if you're not conventionally good-looking, you possess an indefinable allure that keeps people guessing and keeps them coming back for more.

And once you launch into entertainer mode, they're completely hooked. Your charm can light a room, and you invariably leave with whichever attractive face caught your attention.

Yet, this year, while having no shortage of admirers, you may find yourself more interested in other matters. Something else has captured your imagination, and you're eager to explore it in more depth.

Single Monkeys are destined to be heartbreakers in 2025. You'll play the field, but you're not really serious. Admirers who get in too deep are likely to be disappointed.

Attached Monkeys, meanwhile, have the potential to deepen their relationship, but only if their partner shares the new Monkey passion.

Together, you can explore whatever it is that has captured the Monkey imagination and grow ever closer as you do so. But should your partner prove indifferent to your new interest, Monkey, it might be time to say goodbye.

Secrets of Success in 2025

In a nutshell, Monkey, the secret of success for you this year is simple. Behave yourself!

The Monkey finances could be set to expand in a big way, and you are a brilliant money manager – thanks to your shrewd brain and the Metal element to which you belong. Metal and money adore each other.

Yet the Snake demands patience and careful consideration in business matters, and the Monkey is not known for these gifts.

The typical Monkey technique is to rush into some exciting venture, cast a shrewd eye over the market or prospects and – on finding them promising – toss the resulting fine print over to someone else to sort out.

True, this does often work, but it also leaves you at the mercy of your expert, who may turn out not to be as competent as you expected. This year, you could come severely unstuck by leaving the boring details to someone else.

Then there's your habit of aiming for shortcuts wherever possible and bending the rules as far as they can possibly stretch. In 2025, they're likely to shatter into a thousand pieces, leaving many a Monkey on the wrong side of the law.

So, this year, adopt your wise Moneky pose, check the small print with care, treat the regulations like a sacred document, and you can't fail.

The Monkey Year at a Glance

January – The Dragon is leaving, just as you were enjoying the ride. Cheer yourself up with a big farewell party.

February – You don't stay down for long. New opportunities are beginning to appear and you like the look of them. Time to explore.

March – A fusspot gets irritating, but you discover a wonderful way to get them on your side.

April – The boss suddenly notices your brilliant talents. About time, too. Promotion could be beckoning.

May – A well-meaning colleague advises you against over-confidence. As if… Annoying, but listen.

June – You have a stalker. Or at least a past love that won't take no for an answer. Maybe you could set them up with someone else?

July – A new venture looks promising. This could be very successful. Time to delve deeper.

August – Monkey finances get a welcome boost. Pay rise or commission or maybe you've won the lottery?

September – An unusual date could work out surprisingly well. You're really too busy for romance, but on the other hand…

October – A spoilsport at work disagrees with your plans. Never mind. Clever Monkey can talk them around.

November – The festive season is approaching, and you're in your element. Top of every guest list, you shine in a crowd.

December – It's champagne all around this Christmas after a surprisingly fabulous year.

Lucky colours for 2025: White, Blue, Gold

Lucky numbers for 2025: 4, 9

Three Takeaways

Stick to the rules

Don't tease the boss

Slow down

CHAPTER 6: THE ROOSTER

Rooster Years

26 January 1933 – 13 February 1934

13 February 1945 – 1 February 1946

31 January 1957 – 17 February 1958

17 February 1969 – 5 February 1970

5 February 1981 – 24 January 1982

23 January 1993 – 9 February 1994

9 February 2005 – 28 January 2006

28 January 2017 – 15 February 2018

13 February 2029 – 2 February 2030

1 February 2041 – 21 January 2042

Natural Element: Metal

Will 2025 be a Golden Year for the Rooster?

So how ya doing, Rooster? If your feathers are a little ruffled and your feet are beginning to ache, it's probably because 2024 was a pretty memorable year for you if you're typical of your sign. You got yourself noticed one way or another, even if you didn't intend to, and you've been busy, busy, busy.

True, various situations may not have been comfortable, and you felt forced to make a stand, but the point is you proved you could do it, and people took you seriously. Which is what the Dragon of 2024 was aiming for. You may not realise it yet, but you're a stronger, more forceful Rooster as a result.

Even so, you're probably feeling a bit jaded as 2025 opens. Completely understandable. Well, the good news is that things will be a lot simpler this year. For a start, you laid much of the groundwork in 2024 and that was the tough part. Now the Snake will help you add the finishing touches, and in a more relaxed fashion.

The other great thing is that you and the Snake are very good buddies. The Snake admires you tremendously, Rooster, and intends to do everything possible to help. Wise Snake realises that beneath your fine plumage, you often lack confidence. Well, this year, unlike the impatient Dragon, the Snake will provide the gentle encouragement that works best for you.

A number of projects that seem to have dragged on far too long, and which were wearing you down, will finally get over the line thanks to the Snake's discreet input.

Once those burdens are out of the way, you're suddenly free to spread your wings, explore other interests and generally enjoy yourself.

Many signs feel the urge to break with the past and change their lives completely this year, Rooster, but if you're typical of your sign, you're unlikely to join them. You've worked hard to get as far as you've managed so far, and you're not going to throw it all away just when your goal is in sight.

So, most Roosters will see their ambitions either fulfilled or draw impressively closer this year. The Rooster career or business will flourish; the Rooster home takes on a new gloss. An extension, a refit, or (at the very least) a lick of paint will transform Rooster surroundings in a very pleasing way.

And the Rooster is in line for a great deal more R&R this year. Why confine yourself to just one holiday, Rooster, when Snake reckons you deserve at least three? Plus a few weekends away in between.

No need to worry about the funds either. Cash is coming your way. It may arrive in stop-start fashion because the expansive energy of the Wood year gets a bit nervous on encountering a Metal creature such as yourself, Rooster. For obvious reasons, Wood is hesitant around metal objects which can be sharp and cutting. So, money will arrive, but you may have to chase various payments to speed up the process.

This slight clash of elements could cause disagreements in the family circle. Many a Rooster will sigh over a loved one's plans, which seem far too big, ambitious, and expensive to be realistic. Refuse to stress over it,

Rooster. Leave them to discover the truth for themselves while settling in to enjoy a fabulous year.

The Wonder of Being a Rooster

Well, of course you look wonderful, Rooster. The typical Rooster believes in putting on a good display. You only get one chance at making a first impression after all, as Rooster would say, so it's only sensible to present yourself in the best possible light.

Rooster may live in the cheapest studio flat and survive on a diet of cornflakes and baked beans, but you'd never know it when seeing them strut down the street – striking and coordinated in stylish, flamboyant outfits, usually fizzing with colour.

The Chinese associate the Rooster with courage, and it's easy to see why. The brave farmyard bird will square up to all-comers armed only with a modest beak, a couple of sharp claws, and a piercing shriek. Yet, Rooster is quite prepared to take on the challenge.

People born under the Rooster sign are just as heroic. Though they may be quaking inside and don't seek out conflict, they can't ignore injustice and will wade in on the side of the underdog if they encounter bullying or unfairness.

Sometimes, this tendency gets them into trouble, particularly if they've misjudged the situation, but Rooster remains undaunted and will wade in just as quickly on the next occasion.

Despite misunderstandings, Roosters are popular characters. They're sociable and chatty and love to be surrounded by friends. Admittedly, when lavished with flattering attention, the Rooster raconteur can exaggerate – sometimes wildly – and this can cause embarrassment later when the reality is revealed. But most signs find this trait rather endearing.

The typical Rooster often aspires to be the boss and usually manages it. They're intelligent and organised but sometimes upset employees with an abrasive manner. Roosters tend to forget they need to choose their words with care.

Yet few people realise that, deep down, Rooster lacks confidence. At some level, they feel not quite as good enough as they are, so they have to make up for that lack of confidence with a grand show, hard work, and fearless deeds. For the same reason, their feelings are easily hurt, though the typical Rooster would never admit it.

The Rooster Home

You're unlikely to be invited to a Rooster home should the Rooster be short of funds. Rooster likes to entertain as lavishly as possible and would loathe being unable to ply guests with tasty treats and delightful beverages. When finances permit, though, guests are welcomed to warm rooms that zing with colour and bristle with the latest gadgets. The Rooster is fascinated by clever labour-saving devices and the most up-to-date, super-sleek technology. Where possible, the Rooster home also looks out onto green space of some kind. Although not necessarily keen on gardening, most Roosters retain a trace memory of country living and find the proximity of grass and trees relaxing. The ideal Rooster home boasts bifold doors opening onto a pleasing vista of plants and flowers, even if they live in the centre of town. They particularly enjoy entertaining out of doors, too, and are not put off by a little inclement weather.

Being Friends with the Rooster

The typical Rooster has a wide circle of friends and acquaintances. Outgoing and sociable, they can strike up a new friendship wherever they happen to be. They are excellent company. Great storytellers with long memories, they can enthral listeners with their amusing tales.

Yet the more you know a Rooster, the more layers you discover. For a start, they can be impulsive in actions and also in words. This leads them to speak out more bluntly than is wise… before they've had time to choose the most… ahem… tactful language.

Consequently, the Rooster has a tendency to fall out with people, too. Admittedly, they make new friends as quickly as they lose the old ones, but many Roosters have a confusingly ever-changing network.

What's more, even if you're not bothered by Rooster's occasional clumsily phrased opinion, Rooster may be bothered by yours. The typical Rooster is surprisingly thin-skinned and can take offence where none was intended.

They find it incredibly easy to misinterpret some innocent remark and will stomp off, deeply wounded by the imagined insult.

The person who understands this is merely a symptom of their feathered friend's lack of confidence will know exactly how to heal Rooster's injured feelings. Manage that and you'll be friends for life.

Rooster Superpowers

Courage

Persistence

Bold action

Best Jobs for Rooster 2025

Mayor

Auctioneer

Farmer

Charity Boss

Supermarket Manager

Fashion Advisor

Perfect Partners

Cupid's arrow can strike anywhere at any time, of course, but once the novelty of new romance wears off, some relationships are easier to maintain than others. Here's a guide to the Rooster's compatibility with other signs.

Rooster with Rooster

Fabulous to look at, though they would be, these two alpha creatures would find it difficult to share the limelight. They can't help admiring each other at first sight, but since both need to be the boss, there could be endless squabbles for dominance. What's more, neither would be able to give the other the regular reassurance they need. Probably not worth attempting.

Rooster with Dog

Rooster and Dog are not the best of partners. Dog can be as plain-spoken as Rooster and is not likely to be impressed by overt behaviour. Moreover, Dog is often critical, and Rooster can't stand criticism. Rooster, on the other hand, is likely to sense and resent Dog's attitude. Frustration abounds for both in this relationship. Only for the hopelessly love-struck.

Rooster with Pig

These two might seem an unlikely couple – modest Pig with extrovert Rooster. Yet Pig has no need or wish to crow and can see the vulnerable character that lurks beneath Rooster's fine feathers; Rooster, meanwhile, responds to Pig's kindness and undemanding nature. As long as Rooster doesn't get bored, this can be a contented relationship.

Rooster with Rat

The first thing Rat notices about the Rooster is its beautiful plumage, but this is a relationship which is unlikely to get much further than initial admiration. Rooster's direct and frank approach can strike the Rat as tactless, while the Rooster can't understand why Rat has to make life so convoluted and complicated. Then again, Rooster's natural confidence and aplomb can come across as bragging to the Rat. These two have to be very determined to make a partnership work.

Rooster with Ox

For all its bravado and showing off, the Rooster is a down-to-earth type, drawn to security and accumulating the good things in life – requirements that Ox understands very well and can supply effortlessly. What's more, Ox can't help but admire Rooster's fine feathers and skill at communicating in a crowd – attributes Ox doesn't have and is unlikely to acquire. These two could enjoy a very good partnership.

Rooster with Tiger

The only feathered creature in the zodiac, the opulence and novelty of Rooster's appearance will draw Tiger like a magnet. What's more – deep down – they are both quite serious-minded types, so on one level, they'll have much to share. Yet, despite this, they're not really on the same wavelength and misunderstandings will keep recurring. Could be hard work.

Rooster with Rabbit

A difficult match. However unfair it seems, Rooster comes over as loud, boastful, and uncouth to Rabbit, while Rabbit appears dull, staid, and insufficiently admiring of Rooster's fine feathers to appeal to Rooster. These two just can't see below the surface of the other, and it would be surprising if they ended up together. Only to be considered by the very determined.

Rooster with Dragon

A Dragon and Rooster pairing will always attract attention. These two are both gorgeous beings and love to be surrounded by admirers. They will probably enjoy going out together and being seen as a couple, but in the long-term, they may not be able to provide the kind of support each secretly needs. Entertaining for a while, but probably not a lasting relationship.

Rooster with Snake

Surprisingly, Snake and Rooster work well together. Both gorgeous in different ways, they complement each other without competing. Snake's keen eyes can see beneath Rooster's proud facade to the sensitive, unsure person inside, while Rooster appreciates Snake's unobtrusive strength and wise words of encouragement at just the right moment. These two could be inseparable.

Rooster with Horse

The eye-catching Rooster intrigues Horse while Rooster appreciates Horse's strength and agility. They can enjoy many stimulating dates together. Yet, in the long run, this couple may not be able to provide the stability the other needs. They're both sensitive types but in different ways. After a while, the relationship could run out of steam.

Rooster with Goat

Peaceful Goat is not one to make feathers fly, so these two are unlikely to fall out, but they're unlikely to find perfect compatibility, either. Goat is unable to give Rooster the regular ego boosts that make Rooster thrive, while Rooster is baffled by Goat's unpredictable devotion to impractical projects or people. Misunderstandings are likely.

Rooster with Monkey

While not a perfect match, these two have got a lot of time for each other. Monkey recognises the intelligent brain beneath Rooster's plumage, while Rooster admires Monkey's ability to entertain a crowd, and they both adore socialising. They could enjoy many fun dates in.

Rooster Love 2025 Style

Take a bow, Rooster – you're looking your dazzling best, and now that some of the stresses of the previous year have melted away, you can shake out those fine feathers and take your rightful place centre stage.

All eyes will certainly be on you, Rooster. Particularly since some of the reflected glory of your mate, the ruling Snake, is adding even more sparkle to your allure. You just can't fail to charm. All you need do is turn up.

What's more, you're ready to make up for lost time, having been too busy for much romance in 2024.

Yet that slightly hesitant Wood energy where Metal signs are concerned (which is influencing the whole year) is likely to affect your love life, too. While all is going well, and you're having a great time, Rooster, there's also an air of indecision.

Maybe you can't choose between two loves, or someone you've set your sights on isn't free just now – either way, it looks like there's no point in trying to rush things. Take your time, Rooster; go with the flow and you'll have a blast.

Attached Roosters are already dusting off the romantic candles and browsing the brochures for cosy breaks 'a deux'. Maybe you feel your partner missed out last year, and you want to spoil them now, Rooster. If that's the case, go for it! Make a big fuss of your other half, and 2025 will be your most loved-up year yet.

Secrets of Success in 2025

With the Snake cheering you on, Rooster, you're all set for success this year. What's more, you won't have to work so hard, and you won't run into too many irritating glitches.

Yet it's still possible to annoy the Snake if you take your good fortune for granted. While the Rooster is quite prepared to put in the hours in the workplace, Snake is not particularly impressed. Snake believes in quality over quantity and encourages careful preparation to ensure the best results rather than long days.

What's more, as fond of you as the Snake is, Rooster's tendency to rush into ventures without sufficient thought aggravates the careful Snake.

So, this year, all you need to do, Rooster, is slow down, delve deeply into every suggestion before committing yourself, and don't take unnecessary risks. Tame that impulsive streak, and you'll cruise through 2025.

The Rooster Year at a Glance

January – You might be a little the worse for wear, Rooster, but you're still willing to party if the rest of the gang are. Ignore the party poopers and enjoy.

February – A rabble-rousing friend suggests joining a protest. Think twice, Rooster.

March – Changes around the homestead are not to your liking. You don't have to agree. Devise your own plan.

April – The boss gives you extra work – but it could lead to promotion. It might be worthwhile.

May – A partner surprises you with a treat. Foreign fields beckon.

June – Summer parties are popping up everywhere. It would be rude not to go.

July – More responsibility comes your way but you meet resistance from a certain quarter. Think diplomacy.

August – Home projects are reaching fruition. You're pleased with the results. Celebrations all around.

September – Looks like some sort of recognition is coming your way. Passed an exam or got that promotion? No harm in more celebrations.

October – A tricky person at work still needs careful handling. You're tempted to speak your mind. Best not to.

November – Not normally your thing, but a bestie fancies a spa break and wants you along. Why not?

December – Everything's looking good on the home front at last. You can now entertain the family with pride. Go for it, Rooster.

Lucky colours for 2025: Gold, Brown, Yellow

Lucky numbers for 2025: 5, 7, 8

Three Takeaways

Don't rush in

Think tact and diplomacy

Act confidently

CHAPTER 7: THE DOG

Dog Years

14 February 1934 – 3 February 1935

2 February 1946 – 21 January 1947

18 February 1958 – 7 February 1959

6 February 1970 – 26 January 1971

25 January 1982 – 12 February 1983

10 February 1994 – 30 January 1995

29 January 2006 – 17 February 2007

16 February 2018 – 4 February 2019

13 February 2029 – 2 February 2030

22 January 2042 – 9 February 2043

Natural Element: Metal

Will 2025 be a Glorious Year for the Dog?

How's it going so far, Dog? Hopefully, you've managed to bag yourself a good long rest over the festive season because life's about to get hectic, and then some. Get ready to release your inner Greyhound.

If you're typical of your sign, the past year has probably not been the easiest, Dog. Blame it on that pesky Dragon of 2024 and the way your two signs just don't understand each other.

Obstacles, family quarrels, and unnecessary difficulties are likely to have blighted the Dog path all year. Despite this, most Dogs – being persistent and determined types – will have battled on through and find themselves in 2025 in a better situation than before.

The good news is that 2025 is set to be a big improvement. This is because the ruling Snake has much more time for you than the Dragon. It's not that you're besties (the relationship is more complicated than that), but at least it's positive.

The typical Dog finds the Snake rather fascinating, if a little scary, while the Snake –aware of Dog's admiration and not averse to it – regards the Dog as useful. So, stand by, Dog, to be inundated with tasks.

The Snake will take advantage of your many gifts, Dog, by showering you with situations that demand just such skills.

For a start, you're a loyal and conscientious worker, so suddenly the boss, or your business venture, finds it's imperative you devote extra hours to your role. More responsibility is likely to be heaped on the typical Dog this year as a result – so the happy side effect is that many a Dog will shoot up the career ladder, even if they didn't set out to do so. You'll enjoy the extra pay that goes with it too, Dog, so what's not to like?

Then there's your well-known devotion to family. Expect that to be called upon to the hilt. To the typical Dog, family is everything. So now your life is likely to be awash with relatives in various forms of need. Broken relationships, unexpected housing difficulties, financial crises – any or all of these issues could be on Dog's agenda this year, as they come running to you with their problems.

The funny thing is, though you may sigh and complain, Dog, deep down you love being needed. In your practical, sensible way, you'll plough through the challenges one by one until a solution is found. You may end up sharing your home with a relative or two for a while, Dog, but you're likely to enjoy the company. All in all, becoming the hub of the family in 2025 will give you immense satisfaction.

Since this is once again a Wood year and you're a Metal creature, last year's stop-start influence on cash and projects is likely to continue, though in a more muted form. This is because Wood has no affinity with Metal. Metal, associated as it is with wood-cutting tools, tends to make Wood back away if at all possible.

In day-to-day life, this can play out as irritating delays to promised payments and annoying hold-ups in other plans. Since Wood energy is expansive, chances are you'll get what you should in the end, but it will involve a tussle. Fortunately, Snake energy is much softer than last year's Dragon power, so these annoying aspects should cause fewer problems.

Many a Dog has been hoping to move to a more suitable home for quite a while now, yet encountered endless hitches and distractions that prevented it happening. Family distractions still feature this year, but ironically may provide the impetus you need to finally make the change. Some Dogs will need bigger premises to accommodate extra family members, while others will downsize to escape them! Either way, you could well find exactly what you're looking for towards the end of the year.

And, finally, the typical Dog can expect an expansion to the family circle. New babies, new pets, new partners… all heading your way to cheer the year.

The Wonder of Being a Dog

You really are something special, Dog. Okay, if you're a typical hound, you're probably the modest type and scarcely even notice the qualities that single you out from other signs. Yet, in your own quiet way, you are admirable.

For some reason, there are cultures that don't respect dogs, but not China. The Chinese regard the zodiac sign of the Dog as a symbol of justice and compassion. Noble, honest, and fair, the true zodiac Dog is an incredibly valuable member of any society.

People born under this sign are the most loyal of friends, family members, and workmates. They will support their 'pack' to the bitter end, even if their own interests suffer as a consequence.

They attach great importance to fairness in every aspect of life, and for this reason, they're great believers in rules.

Even if they encounter a rule they don't like, they will follow it anyway – because they believe if everyone had a pick-and-choose attitude to which rules they obeyed, civilisation would collapse. The Dog is quite prepared to set a good example, even in the face of scorn from other signs.

Basically, the Dog is the most honest of all the signs. You can rely on Dog to do the right thing – always. Typical Dog is the one that hands back excess change when the shop assistant makes a mistake, notifies the bank if too much cash is credited to their account, and never fiddles a penny on any expenses they're allowed. For these reasons, other signs instinctively trust the Dog, even if they don't realise why.

Dogs make excellent workers, of course, and excel in management. As well as being intelligent, honest, and brave, their quest for fairness ensures they always give a fair day's work for whatever they're paid.

Determined not to 'cheat' the boss, they usually end up doing far more than is necessary.

Yet employers are often baffled by their Dog staff. They mistake devotion and conscientiousness for driving ambition and can't understand, therefore, why the typical Dog seems uninterested in climbing the career ladder or competing for promotion. They assume Dog hasn't grasped the necessary methods when, in fact, the Dog is just more interested in what's going on at home.

Deep down, every Dog is longing to belong to a pack. Once they've found one and settled in, they're happy and content and – if necessary – will sacrifice themselves for the wellbeing of the others. And should a crisis occur, the typical Dog will be on the case instantly, probably leading the rescue party.

The Dog Home

The great thing about the Dog home is that it's a genuine home, not an interior design project. The typical Dog motto tends to be: 'You'll have to take me as you find me.'

They mean it too, so visitors need to be prepared for a lively melange of children, dogs, cats, and smaller pets of the moment, plus the detritus of various family hobbies and sports.

Furnishings are likely to be comfortable, well-worn, and scattered with pet hair, toys, and the occasional pet. Flooring sports muddy prints, paw or foot, the odd bowl of water, and more toys: dog, child or both. The wallpaper may be starting to fade, but it hardly shows, covered as it is in kid's artwork and family photos.

Yet despite the slightly chaotic air, there's a happy atmosphere, and the Dog is a welcoming host. Guests are greeted warmly and pressed to stay for copious home-cooked snacks and huge mugs of whatever Dog is brewing. Visitors end up staying far longer than they intended and helping with the washing up, too.

Being Friends with the Dog

Anyone lucky enough to be friends with the Dog has a loyal mate for life. You can depend on Dog to be on your side, even when you're wrong. Dog will give you their last penny if you're in need and will turn up with soup, flowers, and something undemanding to read if you're sick. They'll feed your pets when you're away and pick up your children from school if you're delayed; it wouldn't even occur to them to ask for anything in return.

Moreover, the ever responsible Dog has a surprisingly carefree side when relaxed. The Dog loves to play. Expect picnics and games and hours of silly fun when Dog's in the mood for some R&R.

The only problem with making such a delightful friend is that it takes a while for Dog to admit new faces to the charmed inner circle. Their friendly manner easily attracts new acquaintances, but they tend to remain acquaintances for quite a while. It takes time for Dog to bestow their trust, but when they do it's unbreakable and unconditional.

The other thing to bear in mind is that Dog's honesty is unflinching. Never ask the Dog if a certain outfit makes you look fat, or a particular colour suits you, unless you really want to know the plain, unvarnished truth. Dog truly doesn't understand why you'd want anything less.

On the other hand, should Dog pay you a compliment, you know – without doubt – it's sincere.

Dog Superpowers

Bravery

Reliability

Competence

Best Jobs for Dog

Police Officer

Paramedic

Nurse

Playgroup Manager

Vet

Accountant

Perfect Partners

Cupid's arrow can strike anywhere at any time, of course, but once the novelty of new romance wears off, some relationships are easier to maintain than others. Here's a guide to the Dog compatibility with other signs.

Dog with Dog

Dogs love company so these two will gravitate to each other and stay there. Both are loyal, faithful types; neither need worry the other will stray. They'll appreciate their mutual respect for doing things properly and their shared love of a stable, caring home. This relationship is likely to last and last. The only slight hitch could occur if, over time, the romance dwindles and Dog and Dog become more like good friends than lovers.

Dog with Pig

In the outside world, the Dog and the Pig can get along well together; in fact, Pigs (being intelligent creatures) can do many of the things dogs can do, so it's not surprising this zodiac pair make a good couple. Good-natured Pig is uncomplicated and fair-minded, which suits Dog perfectly. Also, Pig brings out Dog's playful side – which delights Pig, who's always keen to have a playmate. A happy relationship involving many restaurants.

Dog with Rat

The Rat and the Dog get along pretty well together. Both are strong characters who respect each other and give each other space when required. But deep down, the Dog is a worrier and gets anxious about unnecessary risks, while Rat just can't help sailing close to the wind if an interesting opportunity presents itself. Long-term, reckless Rat might unintentionally drive Dog to distraction. Only to be considered by Dogs with nerves of steel.

Dog with Ox

These two ought to get along well as they're both sensible, down to earth, loyal, hardworking, and in tune with each other's basic beliefs. And yet, somehow, they don't. Dog has a playful streak and finds this lacking in Ox, while Ox may be baffled by what seems like pointless silliness in Dog. If they can agree to differ, they could make a relationship work.

Dog with Tiger

While not exactly opposites, these two are different enough to intrigue each other yet similar enough in basic outlook to get on well. Both Tiger and Dog are idealistic and uninterested in material gain, yet where Dog can be nervous, Tiger is bold. And where Tiger attracts controversy, Dog will be loyal. This partnership could be lasting and valuable.

Dog with Rabbit

Despite the fact that in the outside world, Rabbit could easily end up as Dog's dinner, the astrological pair gets on surprisingly well. Dog appreciates Rabbit's careful, efficient ways and soft voice, while Rabbit admires Dog's energy and good intentions. Dog's lack of interest in the finer points of interior design might try Rabbit's patience, but with a little work, these two could reach an understanding.

Dog with Dragon

Not the easiest of combinations. Down-to-earth Dog can't see what all the fuss is about when it comes to Dragons. Unimpressed by glamour and irritated by what seems (to Dog) the gullibility of Dragon admirers, Dog can't be bothered to find out more. Dragon, meanwhile, is hurt by Dog's lack of interest. Great determination would be needed to make this work.

Dog with Snake

Some snakes seem to have an almost hypnotic power, and for some reason, Dog is particularly susceptible to these skills. We've heard of snake charmers, but snakes can be dog charmers, and without even trying, Snakes can find themselves the recipients of Dog devotion. Since the Dog is strong, loyal, and can be fun, Snake is not averse to this but might, in the end, find it boring.

Dog with Horse

Both are good friends of man; these two can make a formidable team. Dog understands the occasional need for solitude while admiring Horse's strength and agility. Horse, meanwhile, senses Dog's loyalty and down-to-earth nature. Both lovers of the great outdoors and physical activity, they'll never be short of adventures to share. A promising long-term relationship.

Dog with Goat

This is another relationship that could be tricky. Loyal Dog would be quite willing to stand by Goat when practical problems loom but could end up irritated by Goat's inability to learn from previous mistakes, and so keeps making them. Goat can't understand why Dog gets so bothered. With care, these two could learn to live together.

Dog with Monkey

Monkey finds Dog intriguing. Monkey senses Dog's strength of character coupled with its playful streak, which fits well with Monkey's love of games. Dog, meanwhile, appreciates Monkey's energy and light-hearted approach. Yet before long, Monkey's disdain for rules will grate on Dog's instinctive love of them. They cannot agree in this area, and it could lead to arguments.

Dog with Rooster

Rooster and Dog are not the best of partners. Dog can be as plain-spoken as Rooster and is not likely to be impressed by overt behaviour. What's more, Dog is often critical, and Rooster can't stand criticism. Rooster, on the other hand, is likely to sense and resent Dog's attitude.

Frustration abounds for both in this relationship. Only for the hopelessly love-struck.

Dog Love 2025 Style

The typical Dog is a fine-looking creature. Strong and healthy looking with beautiful eyes and fabulous hair. Single Dogs tend not to be slaves to fashion and prefer casual clothes, yet they somehow evolve their own striking style that other signs just can't emulate.

So, you'll not be short of admirers in 2025, Dog, yet romance could get complicated all the same. Family dramas have a nasty habit of hindering any number of hot dates. Either you'll be called away mid-proceedings to rescue a relative in distress, or you'll have to cancel altogether and hope you can reschedule.

Then there's the possibility that, for once, sensible single Dog will fall for some wildly unsuitable love. Maybe they're already attached, maybe they're not interested, or maybe it's simply that the two of you don't really get on. Whatever the reason, Dog, your friends are likely to warn you off, and you'll likely take no notice.

It may not end well, but you need to find that out for yourself. Then, you'll chalk it up to experience.

Attached Dogs could find the same type of family issues mar date nights with their partners. It helps if your partner's family is just as demanding as your own. The two of you can commiserate together. But if your beloved feels you always put your family before them, there could be trouble. Tread carefully.

Secrets of Success in 2025

Success is not actually a secret this year, Dog. It's more or less forced on you.

You're not aiming to be super busy, you weren't planning to put in extra hours at work, and you certainly didn't intend to devote most of your free time to untangling family disputes. Yet this is what's likely to become necessary for the typical Dog during the reign of the Snake, and in being such a good-natured, helpful character, you just can't refuse.

Yet it's not bad news, despite your initial reluctance. All that hard work will pay off big time, Dog, in every department. Your career will enjoy a massive boost, as will your bank balance, and your family will be ever grateful – which makes you happy.

Just try to sweeten that gruff tongue around your more nervous colleagues. Not everyone understands your bark is worse than your bite when you're under stress. At work, stay calm, smile politely, and keep your frank opinions to yourself, and you'll be the toast of 2025.

The Dog Year at a Glance

January – It's a bit of a slog after the festive season, and you're not keen to get moving. Duty calls, though, and Dog answers.

February – You've hit your stride now. There's a lot to do.

March – Someone in your circle is checking out house moves. Time to go visit properties with them.

April – A row is brewing in the workplace. You're not directly involved, but you're tempted to have your say. Think tact, Dog.

May – An intriguing text captures your attention. Are they flirting with you?

June – A past love reappears. Is it really all over between you, or can the sparks fly again? Time to find out...

July – A family member arrives with a practical problem. You know just who to call.

August – A big family get-together materialises, and you're in your element. You'll end up in charge, Dog.

September – An individual you never liked is being unpleasant to one of your besties. You're bound to steam in but don't overdo it.

October – Some idiot at work is trying to stir up trouble. They're jealous of your reputation, Dog. Don't be played.

November – Young people in your orbit come to you for advice, and you're flattered. Enjoy imparting words of wisdom.

December – How you love the festive season. You've bought far too many gifts, and not everyone likes board games, but you're determined to play anyway. Fun all around.

Lucky colours for 2025: Purple, Jade, Yellow

Lucky numbers for 2025: 3, 4, 9

Three Takeaways

A white lie is not a sin
Don't work too hard
Make time for romance

CHAPTER 8: THE PIG

Pig Years

4 February 1935 – 23 January 1936

22 January 1947 – 9 February 1948

8 February 1959 – 27 January 1960

27 January 1971 – 14 February 1972

13 February 1983 – 1 February 1984

31 January 1995 – 18 February 1996

18 February 2007 – 6 February 2008

5 February 2019 – 24 January 2020

23 January 2031 – 10 February 2032

10 February 2043 – 29 January 2044

Natural Element: Water

Will 2025 be a Glorious Year for the Pig?

The brilliant thing about you, Pig, is that you get on with almost all the signs. Not only is this an agreeable way to move around the world, but it also means that – for most years – you're unlikely to run into trouble from that year's ruler.

In 2024, you benefited from a smiling Dragon that finds the inoffensive little Pig rather cute. No year is perfect, of course, but the doting Dragon will have eased your path wherever possible.

Unfortunately, the Snake of 2025 is not so indulgent. The Snake has nothing against you personally, Pig; it just doesn't quite see the point of many of your Piggy aims and ambitions. So don't expect any special favours from the serpent.

This is not necessarily a bad thing, Pig. You may have become a little lazy in the past few years, which might have been restful but certainly didn't benefit you long term. In 2025, you get the chance to sharpen up and raise your game. This could be the making of you, Pig.

While you may not be the Snake's number one companion, it's another matter with the Wood element of the year. The Pig is a Water creature, and Wood adores Water. Water is essential for Wood to grow, therefore, your contribution is always welcome. This doesn't go down too well with the Snake, of course, which is a Fire animal at heart and we all know what Fire thinks of Water – so there's a bit of a battle going on throughout your year.

This may play out in a stop/start feel to 2025, Pig, with plans made and then postponed, important letters lost in the post, and people changing their minds on you at the last minute. But, more interestingly, it could also materialise as an unexpected person becoming highly significant in your life.

Many Pigs could find themselves going into partnership with someone they don't especially take to, and yet the two of you, by some strange alchemy, work amazingly well together.

Neither of you understands it, but your combined efforts produce spectacular results. Much better than either of you could achieve on your own.

This partnership could involve a new business or perhaps it's a strategic alliance at work or even a combining of forces on the domestic front – but once it gets going, Pig, it could transform your life.

No one will be more amazed by this relationship than you; just don't expect it to be serene. The demands of Wood can be exhausting for Water, and you'll be rushed off your feet at times. At others, your partner's attitude could seem distressingly abrasive and you have to struggle to avoid a row. It's not easy, yet the end results will be worth the huge effort.

Many a Pig will hope to recharge at home. This is probably not the best time to launch into massive renovations, but you could be inspired to draw up plans and browse a few shops for ideas to be followed up when life is quieter.

And on the R&R front, many a Pig circle will be enlivened by a new wave of little piglets. Few things please the typical Pig more than cuddling little ones and hitting the stores to buy tiny outfits and exciting toys. Fortunately, cash is rolling your way too this year, Pig, so you can afford to splurge. You're going to love it.

The Wonder of Being a Pig

There are so many wonderful things about you, Pig, it's difficult to know where to start.

Yet, in the West, the Pig is often regarded at best as a figure of fun, and at worst as an insult. Jokes around over-eating, messy homes, or grubby habits abound; the zodiac Pig has to develop a good sense of humour to cope.

Fortunately, this isn't difficult as the typical Pig is the most amiable of personalities. Pig is quite prepared to laugh along with everyone else and rarely takes teasing personally.

Attitudes are quite different in the East. The Chinese regard the Pig as a lucky sign, symbolic of abundance and prosperity. Maybe it's something to do with the healthy Pig's lavish amount of flesh or its miraculous fertility that can produce 14 little piglets in one litter. No family, it is believed, can be poor if it's fortunate enough to own a pig.

Zodiac Pigs are neither aggressive nor competitive, so they have no enemies among the other celestial animals. They get on with almost everyone. In fact, few people actually dislike the Pig – the worst the pig ever endures is indifference. Or possibly mild irritation.

People born under this sign are naturally happy. They're tolerant and easy going and see the best in everyone. They're also generous and sympathetic, so they tend to be suckers for hard luck stories. What's more, they'll be taken in again and again by the same person because they believe everyone should be given the benefit of a second chance.

The Pig is only human, of course, and can occasionally be roused to anger but such outbursts are rare.

The most important thing to the Pig – absolutely central to Pig's philosophy – is that life is about having a good time. The Pig just wants to be happy and desires everyone else to be happy, too.

What's more, the Pig finds happiness in the simplest of things. You don't need to spend a fortune to cheer the Pig up or lay on a host of adrenalin-boosting pursuits. The Pig is delighted by cream cakes, freshly baked bread, and chocolate galore – in fact, tasty food of any kind.

Pigs love to laugh, go out dancing, or just lie in the sun.

This is an immensely sensuous sign. Velvet and cashmere, the feeling of grass beneath bare feet, or the scent of spring flowers – these are the things that make the Pig's day.

You're unlikely to find the Pig slogging around a marathon course or taking up rock climbing. Strenuous sports are not the typical Pig's thing. Shopping, however, is a different matter. The Pig is a champion shopper. If shopping was an Olympic sport, Pig would win gold every time.

It's not that Pig is greedy; it just can't resist pretty things and tends to find them on every expedition. Which is where other signs sometimes get irritated with the Pig. The Pig is notoriously bad with money and can't help overspending. Discipline is not a strong point when it comes to cash and food.

Fortunately, most Pigs are highly intelligent, do well at work, and are not normally short of cash. It's just the more they earn, the more lovely things they think they can buy.

The Pig Home

Pig has heard the expression 'less is more' but doesn't quite get it. What is the point of having less of the things you like, Pig wonders, when you could have more? Who would willingly do such a thing? Should you find Pig in a minimalist home, chances are it belongs to someone else and Pig can't wait to move.

The real Pig home tends to be comfortable and warm and overflowing with 'objects'. Pig does a lot of shopping and the resulting treasures have to be proudly displayed throughout Pig's quarters. Many Pigs are great collectors, too, anything from Royal Doulton China to Art Deco bronzes, from ancient stamp collections to vintage clothes. The Pig delights in tracking down the perfect pieces, and one is not enough.

Inside the Pig palace, you're spoiled for novelty scatter cushions and jungles of pot plants, while the kitchen is so well equipped with every conceivable gadget it would make MasterChef envious.

Most true Pigs are excellent cooks and they believe in quality *plus* quantity when it comes to meals. Visitors lucky enough to be invited to dinner are guaranteed a memorable feast.

Being Friends with the Pig

The typical Pig has a great many friends and it's not difficult to see why. The Pig enjoys company, is an uncritical companion, and is quite happy to fall in with whatever the others want to do as long as it's not too strenuous.

What's more, the Pig is always on the lookout for innocent fun, and has a knack for turning the most unpromising situation into a jolly adventure. You'll invariably end up enjoying yourself on jaunts with the Pig.

In fact, the only downside to having a piggy friend is that you're likely to put on weight – any time is the perfect time for coffee and cakes or a cheeky G&T as far as Pig's concerned – or you'll end up broke from all those shopping expeditions.

It takes a great deal of discipline to be friends with the Pig, but most mates reckon it's worth it.

Pig Superpowers

A sunny nature

Kind heart

Unlimited capacity for fun

Best Jobs for Pig

Chef

Wedding Planner

Antiques Expert

Event Manager

Public Relations Consultant

Youth Worker

Perfect Partners

Cupid's arrow can strike anywhere at any time, of course, but once the novelty of new romance wears off, some relationships are easier to maintain than others. Here's a guide to the Pig's compatibility with other signs.

Pig with Pig

When one Pig sets eyes on another Pig, they can't help moving closer for a better look, and should they get talking they probably won't stop. These two understand each other and share so many interests and points of view they seem like a perfect couple. Yet, long-term, they can end up feeling too alike. Pigs rarely argue, yet oddly enough, they can find themselves squabbling over trivialities with another Pig. Care needed.

Pig with Rat

It's very easy for Rat to be beguiled by the Pig. Pig's easy-going, sympathetic nature immediately relaxes the Rat. What's more, Pig loves shopping as much as Rat so the two of them could enjoy many happy expeditions together. Conflict could occur through overspending. Pig does not understand Rat's compulsion to bag a bargain. Pig will buy whatever the price and the two could end up arguing over money.

Pig with Ox

Delightful Pig will catch Ox's eye, and since Pig isn't a constant thrill-seeker, the two of them could enjoy many peaceful evenings together, perhaps over a tasty meal. Yet Pig's spendthrift ways – at least in Ox's eyes – could soon prove very annoying as well as illogical to the Ox, while Pig could find Ox's attitude judgemental and upsetting. Not ideal for the long term.

Pig with Tiger

Carefree Pig will love to bask in Tiger's impressive aura, while Tiger will feel good about protecting this charming but unworldly creature. They enjoy each other's company and Tiger, so focused on lofty matters, will find Pig's compulsive shopping too trivial to worry about. This couple could do well together as long as Pig's fondness for cosy nights in doesn't make Tiger feel trapped.

Pig with Rabbit

Pig is not quite as interested in fine dining as Rabbit, and is happy to scoff a burger as much as a cordon bleu creation, but their shared love of the good things in life makes these two happy companions. Once again, Pig's spending habits might irritate Rabbit, but not too much as Rabbit is quite willing to splurge on lovely things for the home. A relationship would work well.

Pig with Dragon

While Dragon and Pig might seem to be opposites, the two of them can create a surprisingly contented relationship. Pig is quite happy for Dragon to fly around doing exciting things as long as Pig is not expected to do much more than admire profusely. Dragon appreciates Pig's uncritical support and makes allowances for Pig's lack of stamina. This couple could live in harmony.

Pig with Snake

Pig and Snake don't have a lot to say to each other. Snake can't be bothered with Pig's endless shopping, and Pig is hurt by Snake's snobbish attitude. They both enjoy the good things in life, so a luxury fling could briefly be fun – a shared spa break might be a good idea – but in the long term, this relationship is probably not worth pursuing.

Pig with Horse

Pig and Horse are good companions. Horse is soothed by easy-going Pig, and Pig is proud to be seen with such an alluring creature as Horse. They don't have a lot of interests in common, but they don't antagonise each other either. They can jog along amicably for quite a while, but in the long term, they may find they each want more than the other can provide.

Pig with Goat

Happy-go-lucky Pig and laid-back Goat make a good pair. They hate to stir up trouble and always look for a peaceful solution to any challenge. Ideally, they'd avoid the challenge altogether. They could be very contented together as long as Pig's spending and Goat's inability to deal with finances doesn't get them into trouble.

Pig with Monkey

On the surface, these two might seem an unlikely couple. Yet Pig enjoys Monkey's fun and humour while Monkey is happy to be admired uncritically. What's more, Monkey's inventive mind can solve any difficulties caused by Pig's spending, and since Monkey can't resist a challenge, the opportunity to retrain Pig or at least find a way to obtain purchases cheaper could help the relationship last.

Pig with Rooster

These two might seem an unlikely couple – modest Pig with extrovert Rooster. Yet Pig has no need or wish to crow, and can see the vulnerable character that lurks beneath Rooster's fine feathers. While Rooster responds to Pig's kindness and undemanding nature. As long as Rooster doesn't get bored, this can be a contented relationship.

Pig with Dog

In the outside world, the dog and the pig can get along well together; in fact, pigs, being intelligent creatures, can do many of the things dogs can do, so it's not surprising this zodiac pair make a good couple. Good-natured Pig is uncomplicated and fair-minded, which suits Dog perfectly. Also, Pig brings out Dog's playful side – which delights Pig, who's always keen to have a playmate. A happy relationship involving many restaurants.

Pig Love 2025 Style

The sexy little Pig always gets an invite to every party. You're such a dependable guest, Pig. You chat to everyone, charm the most taciturn wallflowers into a smile, and fill the room with your infectious sense of fun. Pig is the one who starts the dancing, hands around the nibbles, and will even help out with the drinks should the host start to flag.

You just love to party, Pig, and other signs are queuing up to party with you. This year, you're as popular as ever, but you may find yourself running into some awkward characters. Single Pigs may even be faced with two or more admirers fighting over their affections.

Amiable Pig doesn't insist on exclusivity and is happy enough to share, but other signs don't always see things the same way. Misunderstandings could develop. It might be best to restrain your enthusiasm a little this year, Pig. Attached Pigs may find their beloved similarly jealous in 2025. Are they feeling insecure, or have you become so engrossed with that new professional partnership that you've not been paying them enough attention? You hate to hurt anyone's feelings. Make a fuss of them, Pig.

Secrets of Success in 2025

Your top tip for 2025, Pig, is to be on the lookout for that unlikely person who's set to become your partner in an important venture. Don't dismiss anyone, no matter how unpromising, at first sight, because the associate you need is not amongst the people you'd normally choose. Chances are the perfect partner will be someone who doesn't necessarily agree with you, and who goes about things in a very un-Pig-like manner. They may seem heartless at times, Pig, and not on your wavelength, but that's kinda the point. You both have completely different strengths, which – together – add up to a formidable combination that will work wonders.

The other point to bear in mind is that once you've got together, they could wear you out, Pig. They may attempt to get you to work harder than you wish. Time to get acquainted with your stubborn inner hog and refuse to be bullied. Once you've charmed this relationship into an agreeable shape, success will blossom.

The Pig Year at a Glance

January – You're not afraid of the approaching Snake, Pig. Making the most of the month and still socialising.

February – A new boss at work arouses much interest. You get on with everyone, so help to make them welcome.

March – A bestie has found a new designer outlet. The Pig coffers are a little low, but it would be rude not to check it out with them.

April – A bold new face arrives in the social circle. It can't hurt to get to know them better.

May – Someone in the family has been let down. You're upset for them. Some choccies or a box of cupcakes might work wonders.

June – Inspiration strikes and a new venture beckons. Do you need a partner or should you go it alone?

July – A friend is looking for a holiday companion. It can't hurt to take a break.

August – One of your favourite times of the year. Non-stop picnics, BBQs, and alfresco meals. The Pig's kitchen is in overdrive.

September – New ventures are proceeding slowly… but proceeding. Ignore criticism and gloomy know-alls.

October – Romance gets complicated. You're being asked to choose. Decisions, decisions.

November – OMG, the shops are full of festive gorgeousness. What is a Pig to do?

December – The Pig home is stuffed with gifts. No room to move. Good thing you're playing Santa all around this year.

Lucky colours for 2025: Gold, Yellow, Orange

Lucky numbers for 2025: 2, 6, 8

Three Takeaways

Open all brown envelopes
Don't be bullied
Ask: do I really need it?

CHAPTER 9: THE RAT

Rat Years

5 February 1924 – 24 January 1925

24 January 1936 – 10 February 1937

10 February 1948 – 28 January 1949

28 January 1960 – 14 February 1961

15 February 1972 – 2 February 1973

2 February 1984 – 19 February 1985

19 February 1996 – 7 February 1997

7 February 2008 – 25 January 2009

25 January 2020 – 11 February 2021

11 February 2032 – 30 January 2033

30 January 2044 – 16 February 2045

Natural Element: Water

Will 2025 be a Glorious Year for the Rat?

Is it too early to crack open the prosecco, Rat? Thought not. Well, you're going to want to celebrate another year when you're one of the winners of the celestial lottery, aren't you? Maybe call up a few friends and make a party of it right now.

The thing is, it's almost unfair, Rat, because you were one of the favourites of 2024 when your good mate the Dragon was in charge. Okay, so chances are you didn't get absolutely everything you hoped for in 2024; nobody ever does. Yet when you look back at your achievements and the events of the previous year, and if you're typical of your sign, you have very little to complain about. You've done pretty well, Rat.

So, it's ironic that you're one of the favoured few once again. You've got a lot to look forward to in 2025, thanks to the incoming Snake. While perhaps not quite so fond of you as the exuberant Dragon, the Snake is nevertheless quite happy to cheer you on and help out with your endeavours.

Many Rats launched new plans last year, not all of which have had time to reach fruition. Well, the good news is the wily Snake has your back and is working behind the scenes to speed up progress. You should see the results you want as the year unfolds.

The other high point is your career, Rat. Your efforts will be noticed and rewarded in a very pleasing fashion during 2025. You're always busy and efficient, but at times in the past, your talents have been overlooked. Not anymore. The Snake admires your work ethic and will make sure everyone else does this year, too.

Entrepreneurial Rats – which is basically all of you, even if you've also taken on a day job – probably dreamed up a new venture last year. What's more, you enjoyed it so much that you're likely to be inspired to add another string to your bow this year. Yet it may require a bit more thought than you expected since the Snake is more cautious than the Dragon and demands much more serious consideration than you needed in 2024.

The other thing to watch out for is that a family member or someone in your circle is so enthused by the Snake's famous propensity to dump the old and wander off to start afresh that they decide to do the same, which will impact on you, Rat.

Strangely enough, the typical Rat, while continually rushing around – enjoying new ventures, new faces, and new deals – doesn't also demand constant changes of scene. Most Rats like to go out to conquer the world from a secure base to which they can scuttle back any time, should things get too tricky on the outside. Once you've found your comfortable nest, Rat, you're not usually in any hurry to change it.

Well, like it or not, Rat, some sort of relocation or at least a radical rethink may be forced on you this year by someone close. You will grumble quite a bit, of course, and moan to all your Ratty friends, but chances are – by the time the Snake slithers away – you'll be very glad you were talked into making the change.

There are bound to be some other challenges during the next 12 months, naturally, despite your favoured position. This is partly due to the fact that, like your cosmic cousin the Pig, you're a Water creature, and this is a Wood year. Plus, of course, the Snake is a Fire sign.

So, there's something of a battle of the elements going on around you. For a start, Wood loves Water because Water helps Wood grow. So, Wood encourages Water creatures with constant opportunities and bids for their attention but can overdo it and end up exhausting them. On the other hand, Fire is understandably nervous of Water and therefore prefers to keep a safe distance.

This could play out in day-to-day life as mouthwatering offers are constantly dangled in front of you, but then turning frustratingly difficult to nail down when you try to grasp them. And since Water also represents emotions, you may be plagued by friends and family suddenly turning unusually fiery and demanding you referee their rows.

Yet none of this will faze you, Rat. Constant motion is your number one demand. You hate to be bored. Well, there's no chance of that in 2025.

The Wonder of Being a Rat

Have you got over it yet, Rat? Discovering the name of your zodiac sign, that is? Not exactly a compliment, you might think. You're not exactly going to boast about being a Rat to your friends, are you?

The flesh and blood creature must be one of the most despised beasts on the planet. No community, probably anywhere in the world, wants a rat on its doorstep. Drastic steps – no matter how horrible – are regarded as necessary by even the gentlest of people to eradicate rats altogether.

Well, clear your mind of all that bad press, Rat, because the zodiac Rat is a different proposition altogether.

The Chinese recognise that while they might not welcome a colony of rats to set up in their homes, the essential energy that animates the Rat is highly admirable.

For a start, the fact that constant efforts to eradicate rodents by humans worldwide always fail demonstrates the Rat's amazing survival skills. The species is immensely successful. Quick, intelligent, and tenacious, they'd be praised for these wonderful qualities if they were human beings.

So, far from being an unfortunate sign, being born in the year of the Rat is regarded as a good omen.

You should have inherited all the positive characteristics of your little furry namesake, Rat, if you're typical of your sign, plus charm, elegance, and good taste.

Few Rats are shy and they are also gregarious, so they have no difficulty popping into a roomful of strangers and instantly striking up a conversation. In fact, the typical Rat relishes just such a challenge.

Mental stimulation of almost any kind is essential for the lively Rat, along with chalking up a victory, since Rat is also the competitive type. For this reason, Rats love shopping and hunting for bargains. The typical Rat seldom pays full price for anything and savours the triumph of the deal probably more than the cut-price item they've just acquired.

Natural entrepreneurs and adventurers, Rats are always on the lookout for business ideas, commercial alliances, and more deals. They never stop. 'The Rat Race' is all a bit of a game to the Rat. In fact, Rat is quite happy to take a risk and finds the element of danger exciting. 'You've got to speculate to accumulate' is one of Rat's favourite sayings, and Rat does a lot of speculating.

Unfortunately, this tendency leads many a Rat into gambling and/or get-rich-quick schemes – often unwisely. Rats can lose money this way, yet they'll do it all again next time around as the thrill is irresistible. And being the great survivors they are, Rats have an uncanny knack for scuttling out of trouble when the going gets tough. They seldom suffer the worst consequences of their disasters.

Above all, family is of immense importance to the typical Rat. While they have a wide circle of friends, family comes first, always. Beneath that easy bonhomie, Rats are shrewd and ambitious – they sail to the top, but – at the end of the day – the rewards are all for their family. If your breadwinner happens to be a Rat, you'll never go hungry.

The Rat Home

Invitations to the Rat home tend to be given out quite regularly. Rat regards home as an ideal place to network and strike deals, as well as the perfect background for stimulating get-togethers and family events.

Rat also has innate good taste and enjoys shopping, so the rodent abode is likely to be fashionable, equipped with the latest technology – acquired at a bargain price – and faintly reminiscent of an upmarket hotel. In fact, the furnishings may well have been bought wholesale from some hospitality supplier.

Between visitors, the Rat home is probably found to be messy and draped with various members of the Rat extended clan: devouring snacks and gaming on Rat's 219-inch TV screen. Rat doesn't mind, though, because the typical rodent is out most of the time, pursuing important Rat business. As long as they muck in and restore order before clients are due, Rat is happy.

Being Friends with the Rat

As long as you're prepared to be one of many, it's easy being friends with the Rat. Rat enjoys mixing business with pleasure, so if you have some professional link or a network that might be useful to Rat, you're likely to be welcomed with particular warmth. Rat is renowned for inviting armies of workmates to the Rat wedding or christening of a rodent child.

A business connection is not essential, though. Rat enjoys company; the more, the merrier. As a Rat friend, you will enjoy generous hospitality, witty conversation, and uproarious evenings out.

The only downside is that the Rat is usually so busy, and get-togethers are frequently postponed. In Rat's world, family and business come first. As long as you can accept second place, it's great to be friends with the Rat.

Rat Superpowers

Quick wit

Shrewd eye for a bargain

Never lost for words

Best Jobs for Rats in 2025

Salesperson – selling anything

Entrepreneur

Motivational Speaker

Estate Agent

Press Officer

Perfect Partners 2025

Cupid's arrow can strike anywhere at any time, of course, but once the novelty of new romance wears off, some relationships are easier to maintain than others. Here's a guide to the Rat's compatibility with other signs.

Rat with Rat

These two are certainly on the same wavelength and share many interests. When their eyes first meet, passionate sparks may fly. This relationship could work very well although, over time, the competitive and ambitious nature of both partners could see them pulling in different directions. What's more, if one should succumb to a weakness for gambling or risky business ventures while the other does not, it will end in tears.

Rat with Ox

Oddly enough, this combination can be surprisingly successful. Frenetic Rat and calm Ox may seem to be opposites but, in fact, Rat can find Ox's laid-back approach strangely soothing. Ox is not interested in competing with Rat and will put up with Rat's scurrying after new schemes with patience. As long as Rat doesn't get bored and has enough excitement in other areas of life, this relationship could be very contented.

Rat with Tiger

The magnificent Tiger will always catch Rat's eye because Rat loves beautiful things, but Tiger's natural element is Wood and Rat's is Water which means that Tiger wears Rat out. What's more, Tiger's not interested in Rat's latest bargain, and Rat doesn't share Tiger's passion for changing the world, yet the attraction is strong. If Rat makes an effort to step back and not get in Tiger's way, they could reach a good understanding.

Rat with Rabbit

Rat finds Rabbit intriguing. Here is an attractive, stylish creature that doesn't feel the need to be pushy or take centre stage yet somehow manages to be at the heart of things. The Rat wants to find out more, while Rabbit is flattered and entertained by witty Rat's attention. These two respect each other, but over the long term, Rat could be too overpowering.

Rat with Dragon

This couple is usually regarded as a very good match. They have much in common, being action-loving, excitement-seeking personalities who hate to be bored. It takes a lot to dazzle Rat, but the Dragon's glamorous aura proves irresistible, while Dragon loves to be admired, so each enjoys being with the other. There could be the odd power struggle as these two are both strong characters, but the magnetism is so powerful they usually kiss and make up.

Rat with Snake

The Snake shares Rat's good taste, and being elegant, sophisticated, and smart will delight Rat at first sight. These two get on very well on an intellectual level but perhaps are better as good friends rather than long-term partners. The Snake's love of basking in the sun for hours strikes Rat as lazy and dull, while Rat's need to rush around doing deals and meeting people seems pointless and wearying to the Snake.

Rat with Horse

Rat and Horse both fizz with energy and they love action and looking good, yet this is not seen as an ideal partnership. Nothing's impossible, of course, but these two will have to work hard to find harmony. The Rat will admire Horse's enthusiasm and cheerful approach but become impatient to discover Horse can also be fiery and emotional. Horse, on the other hand, can find Rat's risk-taking behaviour extremely worrying.

Rat with Goat

The Rat is charmed by carefree Goat and fascinated by its artistic talent and happy knack of living in the present. Easy-going Goat tends to like everyone, so is perfectly content to enjoy Rat's company. These two can get along fine, yet they don't really understand each other deep down. Long-term, the Rat may find Goat's lack of interest in the practical side of life, such as finances and bills, irritating.

Rat with Monkey

Unlikely as it might appear, mischievous Monkey and the clever Rat make a good partnership. Their quick minds, sociable natures, and love of novelty ensure that they're never bored together. True, Rat might sometimes feel Monkey is too inclined to skim over the surface of things and could do with being more serious at times, but Monkey's ingenuity and audaciousness always save the day. Both can have a weakness for gambling, though, so need to take care.

Rat with Rooster

The first thing Rat notices about the Rooster is its beautiful plumage, but this a relationship which is unlikely to get much further than initial admiration. Rooster's direct and frank approach can strike the Rat as tactless, while the Rooster can't understand why Rat has to make life so convoluted and complicated. Then again, Rooster's natural confidence and aplomb can come across as bragging to the Rat. These two have to be very determined to make a partnership work.

Rat with Dog

The Rat and the Dog get along pretty well together. Both are strong characters, and they respect each other and give each other space when required. But deep down, the Dog is a worrier and gets anxious about unnecessary risks, while Rat just can't help sailing close to the wind if an interesting opportunity presents itself. Long-term, reckless Rat might unintentionally drive Dog to distraction. Only to be considered by Dogs with nerves of steel.

Rat with Pig

It's very easy for Rat to be beguiled by the Pig. Pig's easy-going, sympathetic nature immediately relaxes the Rat. What's more, Pig loves shopping as much as Rat so the two of them could enjoy many happy expeditions together. Conflict could occur through overspending. Pig does not understand Rat's compulsion to bag a bargain, while Rat can't fathom why Pig is prepared to pay whatever's asked. However, with compromise on both sides, this could work well.

Rat Love 2025 Style

When you're on good form, Rat, in a room full of people, you fizz and sparkle like the finest champagne.

It's unfair really, because you don't need good looks when you've got enough charm to light a small city, but if you're typical of your sign, you're also outrageously gorgeous, too.

No surprise then that the single Rat never lacks for romance – or at least for romantic partners. Yet you're in no hurry to settle down if you're typical of your sign, Rat. For a start, you know you can pick and choose, so you can afford to be picky. And, deep down, family is so important to you that if you're going to make things permanent, you need to find a partner the Rat clan appreciates as much as you do. Not necessarily easy.

Yet flirty Rat never lets on, so admirers often retreat in disappointment, unsure why the relationship failed to progress.

2025 brings even more amorous adventures for the single Rat. Some in unexpected places. Holiday romance or workplace dalliances are especially enjoyable. Will they last? Are they wise? Only you can say, Rat. But you're certainly not going to be bored.

Attached Rats could be in for a surprise with their beloved this year. Your other half is making unexpected demands, and you're not sure you want to agree. Go along with it to keep the peace, Rat. It might turn out better than you expect.

Secrets of Success in 2025

As the famous winner of the Imperial river race and the first animal in the celestial cycle, you're used to doing well, Rat. Failure is not an option, and you seldom experience it. Even if things go wrong, you're the master of the improvised escape route, and you have an amazing knack for reversing awkward situations to your advantage.

2025 is no exception, of course, Rat. Particularly when you have the clever Snake on your side. The only problem is that Snake's approach is almost the opposite of your own.

The Snake wins by stealth, silently watching and waiting and weighing up the situation until the perfect moment. Then it strikes, seemingly at the speed of light, and disappears, leaving onlookers dazed.

That's not your way, Rat. You tend to rush around, chatting to everyone, asking a hundred questions, making new friends, and bartering shamelessly. Sometimes, you enjoy bartering so much that you carry on and on until you wind up with a deal you find you don't even really want.

The Snake doesn't find this amusing. The Snake believes in conserving energy and only putting in effort where it's strictly necessary.

So, your secret of success this year, Rat, is to hone your Snakelike skills. When an idea strikes, be still. Silently assess the situation. Assess it some more. Do your own research. Don't involve other people, and don't talk about it to everyone you meet. When you're absolutely sure – run through it all again.

There's no need to worry you'll lose out to someone else by delaying. With the Snake on your side, your diligence will be rewarded.

Slow down to speed up, Rat, and 2025 will be amazing.

The Rat Year at a Glance

January – The Rat home needs some TLC after the festivities. Dull but necessary, Rat. Roll up your sleeves.

February – Friction at work could be irritating. The famous Rat charm smooths the waters.

March – A young person in the family could do with some mentoring. You're too busy, but then you're always too busy. Reschedule, Rat.

April – A triumph at work has your name all over it, Rat. The boss is delighted and notices your efforts for once.

May – A sexy stranger passes you by. You might just happen to be going in the same direction. Might as well check them out.

June – Someone in your circle is considering a big change. You're not sure this is a good idea. Will they listen?

July – A new project comes your way. It's not your usual field and requires imagination, but you're intrigued. It could work.

August – Summer hi-jinks are overdue; all work and no play is too dull for Rat. A big get-together makes memories.

September – A rival at work sparks your competitive streak. Nothing personal, but you can't let them win.

October – Looks like you've broken the rules, Rat. Ok, bent them slightly. Time to make amends.

November – Spending has got out of hand in the Rat household. Annoying, but maybe you should budget a bit?

December – Everyone's round to Rat's for the festivities. You're working right up to the big day, but throw yourself into the fun. You can sleep next year!

Lucky colours for 2025: Navy, Gold and Lime

Lucky numbers for 2025: 2, 3

Three Takeaways

Think before you speak

Don't rush

Hang onto your cash

CHAPTER 10: THE OX

Ox Years

25 January 1925 – 12 February 1926

11 February 1937 – 30 January 1938

29 January 1949 – 16 February 1950

15 February 1961 – 4 February 1962

3 February 1973 – 22 January 1974

20 February 1985 – 8 February 1986

8 February 1997 – 27 January 1998

26 January 2009 – 13 February 2010

12 February 2021 – 31 January 2022

31 January 2033 – 18 February 2034

17 February 2045 – 5 February 2046

Natural Element: Water

Will 2025 be a Glorious year for the Ox?

Well now, Ox. You're looking good, and you can afford to let that anxious expression slip from your face. Yeah, we can all see it; you're not fooling anyone! The truth is, it's not necessary now.

That huge, fire-breathing Dragon of 2024 has flown away and – once the smoke has cleared – you're going to love what you see. The Snake of 2025 has cleared a beautiful Ox-perfect path for you, all grassy and daisy-strewn, and you can wander at your own pace into a year you're going to enjoy.

Despite your nerves, last year, Ox, if you were typical of your sign, things didn't go badly at all. Though the Dragon is brasher and noisier than you like, and races around far too fast in your opinion, the Dragon has a lot of time for you.

Dragon's main concern last year was to help you make the most of yourself. Admittedly, this could have been uncomfortable for a sensitive creature such as yourself, Ox. Just because you're big and strong, people don't realise you're easily bruised. The Dragon's assistance can be over-boisterous to the point of pain at times.

Yet, here you are now. You've survived. Your prospects are looking good thanks to the Dragon's attentions, and now you have a great year ahead. The Snake is much more your kind of sign, Ox.

Despite the huge difference in size, the two of you have a lot in common. You both prefer to take things slowly, think things through, and not waste energy unnecessarily. The Snake approves of the way you do everything with care, and like you, loves to bask in the sun whenever the opportunity presents itself.

So, this year, the Snake has laid on wonderful career progress – without as much effort as was required in 2024. You can allow yourself to coast (just a little, Ox) and let the praise roll in.

The Snake and the Dragon often have the same goals, Ox, so the eventual outcome should be what the Dragon originally had in mind. Yet, the Snake's way of operating is much more suited to your personality.

Business Oxen will find clients flowing to their door; employed Oxen will delight the boss with ease. You may not even know what you did that was so brilliant, Ox, but just grin and look modest. Many Oxen will find themselves wafted into promotion without even trying.

There's also a very good chance that a long-held ambition will be fulfilled in 2025.

It just gets better and better for you, Ox. This is set to be an excellent year for your finances. Cash is pouring your way, and some of it will likely be unexpected and unearned. A win, an inheritance, a gift, a rebate, or even the sale of some item you'd forgotten you still owned; wherever it comes from, money has your name on it in 2025.

Should any slight struggles ripple the smooth surface of your year, Ox, it will probably be because this is another Wood year (like last year), and you belong to the Water tribe. Wood enjoys the company of Water types since Wood needs Water to grow. So, there's no antagonism between you; it's just that Water creatures like the Ox can find Wood years literally draining, though they can't quite put their finger on why.

The result is likely to be that every aspect of the Ox life feels as if it's expanding in all directions at a dizzying rate.

Expansion is usually a good thing, but when it happens too quickly, it's difficult to assimilate. This year, the Snake will help slow things down for you, but the changes could still be a little unsettling.

Then there's the fact that the Snake belongs to the Fire tribe, and despite Snake's personal fondness for you, Ox, Fire creatures are not natural fans of Water. In day-to-day life, this could play out as far too many temperamental people cross your path, expecting you to reorganise or reroute – when you have no intention of doing so. You really can't be doing with hysterical attention-seekers at the best of times, Ox. You're the patient type, but you have your limits. Just don't let them spoil a wonderful year.

The Wonder of Being an Ox

Anyone who thinks being a zodiac Ox sounds a bit boring needs to think again.

Number two in the celestial River race – and only beaten to first place at the very last minute by the crafty rat – the essential, all-important Ox is highly regarded by the Chinese.

Never dismiss the Ox as simply a big cow with extravagant horns. In years gone by, the Ox was revered. It was thought so precious that it was viewed as a gift from the Gods. Rural life depended on the strength and endurance of the family Ox or Oxen if they were fortunate enough to have two. The beasts made a miraculous difference to farmwork and heavy jobs around the village. The community couldn't manage without them.

People born in the year of the Ox are renowned for similar qualities. In fact, it's believed in some quarters, that every workplace should have at least one Ox on board to ensure success. If you're typical of your sign, Ox, you're not all outward show and silly chatter. You embody serious, invaluable, genuine quality. You don't need to big up your worth or employ PR experts to polish your image. Your actions speak for themselves.

Oxen have a wonderful knack for planning a sensible, logical course to wherever they want to go and then following it, relentlessly, step by step, until they get there, no matter what obstacles they encounter en route. Oxen find it rather puzzling that other people can't seem to adopt the same, simple approach. They don't understand why some signs give up before reaching their goal. Why do they waste their time chopping and changing and getting nowhere, wonders the Ox.

The stamina and endurance of the typical Ox is almost magical. People born under this sign can, if essential, work all through the night, pause for a quick shower and snack, and then go right back to the task. They'll do the same thing again the next night if the job demands it. And the next. Where other signs would crumble and break down, the Ox just plods on, impervious.

These people are the marathon runners of the universe. They are not built for speed, but then they don't need to be. They leave all that frenetic activity to the Monkey and the Rat. Sometimes, it's only patience and tenacity that will get a job done – and that's when only an Ox will do.

Okay, so you're not quite perfect, Ox. Who is? You're not known for your rapier wit or hilarious sense of humour. Though you enjoy a laugh as much as anyone, you're not permanently preparing the next joke or searching for the ironies of life. Survival is a serious business as far as you're concerned, and you intend to survive.

Then, you must admit, Ox, you can be stubborn. Call it tenacious if you like, and – of course – tenacity is a virtue, but it has to be said that when you make up your mind and dig your heels in, it would take dynamite to get you to budge.

Yet the Ox is genuinely honest, kind, and sincere, and not at all materialistic. In fact, the typical Ox is a born craftsman. People born under this sign will labour for hours for little financial gain, simply for the satisfaction of a job well done.

Finally, it takes a lot to seriously annoy the Ox, but when Ox gets mad, people tend to run. The Ox in a temper is a genuinely fearsome sight. Take cover. Better still, just don't go there.

The Ox Home

You have to know the Ox pretty well before being invited to the Ox home. The typical Ox is intensely private and wouldn't dream of inviting just anyone to their sanctuary. Get inside, though, and you will find a comfortable yet practical space filled with natural materials such as leather, wood, and stone. Bare of fripperies such as china ornaments, scented candles, and ruffled curtains, the Ox home may nevertheless be enlivened by some of Ox's own craftwork. Who knew Ox was so artistic? Carved driftwood, intricate collages, chunky jewellery, fused glass coasters – the Ox has mastered them all. Ox boasts green fingers, too, so sunny windowsills will be a tapestry of leaves and twigs as the latest Ox plant cuttings get underway. Just make sure you take a warm sweater when you visit. The temperature at the Ox home is kept notoriously low. Ox just doesn't feel the cold.

Being Friends with the Ox

It can take months, or even years, to be admitted to the Ox circle of trusted friends – which is usually tiny. This is because the typical Ox is a private, highly self-sufficient type. Ox has no need for dozens of different personalities jostling around. While the Ox is affectionate and enjoys company, this sign doesn't require constant companionship. Quiet 'me time' to recharge the Ox batteries is essential, plus the Ox is quite happy to be alone for extended periods. Yet, once admitted to the Ox group of special mates, you'll enjoy a loyal, caring friend who is keen to interest you in their latest artistic hobby or treat you to a mammoth picnic, ideally near water. On rare days off, the Ox loves to laze under the willows on a riverbank or make camp in the sand dunes of some wild beach. Just don't be offended if Ox is working too hard to socialise often, and be prepared for some surprisingly blunt comments. Ox doesn't understand sugar-coating reality and is notoriously plain-spoken. Yet adjust to the eye-wateringly frank Ox-speak, and you'll have a friend for life.

Ox Superpowers

Vast strength – both physical and mental

Stamina

Patience

Best Jobs for Ox 2025

Jeweller

Locksmith

Market Gardener

Florist

Accountant

Perfect Partners

Cupid's arrow can strike anywhere at any time, of course, but once the novelty of new romance wears off, some relationships are easier to maintain than others. Here's a guide to the Ox's compatibility with other signs.

Ox with Ox

These two could be very happy together, as long as one of them plucks up the courage to admit they're interested. Sloppy, sentimental romance is not their style, and they both share this view so there'll be no misunderstandings around Valentine's Day. They know that still waters run deep, and they can enjoy great contentment without showy declarations of love.

Ox with Tiger

Not an easy match. Ox and Tiger could be on different planets. Fiery Tiger doesn't frighten Ox, and Tiger may admire Ox's strong, good looks and sincere nature, but they both need different things from life. Tiger wants to dash about changing the world for the better, while Ox reckons you get more done by buckling down where you happen to be and attending to the details. Clashes could abound.

Ox with Rabbit

Ox finds Rabbit rather cute and appealing. Whether male or female, there's something about Rabbit's inner fluffiness that brings out Ox's highly developed protective instincts. Rabbit meanwhile loves the Ox's reassuring presence and the sense of security Ox provides. These two could get on very well together as long as refined Rabbit can overlook Ox's occasional down-to-earth – Rabbit might say 'coarse' - observations.

Ox with Dragon

Chalk and cheese, though this pair may appear to be, there's a certain fascination between them. Ox may not approve of Dragon's showy manner but recognises Dragon's good intentions, while Dragon admires Ox's strength of character and gift for completing tasks. If each could find a way to tolerate the other's wildly different lifestyles, they might be good for each other, but in the long term, Dragon's hectic pace might wear even the Ox's legendary stamina.

Ox with Snake

Like Ox, the Snake is quietly ambitious and not given to racing around unless it's absolutely necessary. Ox, on the other hand, respects Snake's clever brain and understated elegance. These two could quickly discover how beneficial an alliance between them would be. They're both happy to give the other space when required but also step in with support when needed. This could be a very successful match.

Ox with Horse

Long ago, on many Western farms, Ox was replaced by the Horse, and it may be that Ox has never forgotten and never forgiven. At any rate, these two, despite both being big, strong animals, are not usually friends. Horse is too flighty and frivolous to interest Ox for long, while Ox's methodical, careful ways will irritate the Horse. Best not to go there.

Ox with Goat

Though these two share artistic natures (even if, in the case of the Ox, they're well hidden), deep down, they don't 'get' one another. Ox may be beguiled at first by Goat's friendly, easy-going manner but then disappointed to discover Goat seems to find everyone equally delightful, even those who are plainly unworthy. Goat, on the other hand, can't understand why Ox won't lighten up more. This relationship would require a lot of effort and compromise.

Ox with Monkey

The naughty Monkey scandalises Ox, but in such an amusing way that Ox can't help laughing. Monkey, on the other hand, is equally amused to find an audience that is so easy to shock. This unlikely pair enjoy each other's company and get on surprisingly well. Yet, right from the start, it's probably obvious to both that a long term relationship couldn't last. A fun flirtation, though, could be a terrific tonic for them both.

Ox with Rooster

For all its bravado and showing off, the Rooster is a down-to-earth type, drawn to security and accumulating the good things in life – requirements that Ox understands very well and can supply effortlessly. What's more, Ox can't help but admire Rooster's fine feathers and skill at communicating in a crowd – attributes Ox doesn't have and is unlikely to acquire. These two could enjoy a very good partnership.

Ox with Dog

These two ought to get along well as they're both sensible, down to earth, loyal and hardworking and in tune with each other's basic beliefs. And yet, somehow, they don't. Dog has a playful streak and finds this lacking in Ox, while Ox may be baffled by what seems like pointless silliness in Dog. If they can agree to differ, they could make a relationship work.

Ox with Pig

Delightful Pig will catch Ox's eye, and since Pig isn't a constant thrill-seeker, the two of them could enjoy many peaceful evenings together, perhaps over a tasty meal. Yet Pig's spendthrift ways – at least in Ox's eyes, could soon prove very annoying as well as illogical to the Ox, while Pig could find Ox's attitude judgemental and upsetting. Not ideal for the long term.

Ox with Rat

Oddly enough, this combination can be surprisingly successful. Frenetic Rat and calm Ox may seem to be opposites, but – in fact – Rat can find Ox's laid-back approach strangely soothing. Ox is not interested in competing with Rat and will patiently put up with Rat's scurrying after new schemes. As long as Rat doesn't get bored and generates enough excitement in other areas of life, this relationship could be very contented.

Ox Love 2025 Style

Should you find the single Ox loitering in some club, chances are they'll have a puzzled look on their face because they're trying to locate the exit and can't work out how they got in here in the first place. The Ox is not one of life's party animals, nor are they natural clubbers either.

If forced to take part in some mass social event, the Ox would much prefer a music festival, where Ox can camp under the stars and soak up some favourite bands.

The way they act, you'd think that any sort of love life was surplus to Ox's requirements. Yet deep down, the Ox is a hopeless romantic. What's more, unknown to the modest Ox, other signs find you highly alluring.

The typical Ox is medium tall, slim yet muscular, with thick, shining hair, beautiful skin and a magnetic aura that draws other signs close. You're authentic, Ox. The real deal and the other signs sense it. Come on, Ox, you must have noticed by now!

Well, this year, with your charms enhanced by the sexy Snake, you're going to attract attention in a big way. Fight them off and make excuses though you may, Ox, in the end, one particular admirer is likely to get through your defences and when they do, you'll be smitten. This could be your soulmate, Ox.

The attached Ox can look forward to a happy year, too.

Just be careful not to get too stubborn should your beloved suggest a plan you may not immediately agree with. This is not the time to dig in those heels. Keep the peace by going with the flow. You never know… you might enjoy it.

Secrets of Success in 2025

Phew! Although a lot went well last year – if you're typical of you sign, Ox – it's left you with a pile of paperwork, a disaster of a diary, and a great many tasks that should have been completed by now but are still (despite your legendary discipline) unfinished.

It's not your fault. No point in beating yourself up about it. There was just too much for anyone to cope with in the orderly fashion you prefer.

The good news, Ox, is that the Snake is on your wavelength and intends to provide you with everything you need to bring order to the chaos. You are actually already a success thanks to last year's efforts. You just can't see it yet with all this muddle confusing the picture.

This year, just concentrate on your unique gift of sorting the tasks into a logical order, and then ploughing through them one by one without distractions until they're complete.

The Snake will give you the time you need. You supply the effort, and by the time you've finished, you'll be amazed. Turns out you're something of a star, Ox! Recognition will be yours this year. Just don't let an annoying underling steal your glory. Watch your back.

The Ox Year at a Glance

January – You like January. All is quiet after the holidays, which gives you time to get on with things without interruption.

February – Uh oh. The pace is cranking up. Someone in authority starts making demands, but not necessarily of you, Ox.

March – Mates are trying to get you to commit to a social event. It's months away. How do you know what you'll be doing that far ahead? Tricky.

April – Work needs your attention. Your colleagues are flagging, but you're going strong. You'll have to help them out.

May – You have an admirer, Ox. Perhaps it needed pointing out to you, but now you're flattered. Maybe a date?

June – A stag or hen do is on the horizon. You're not keen, but your arm is twisted. Expensive, of course, but it might be fun, Ox.

July – An artistic event you've always fancied arrives. Of course you've got time; give it a try.

August – Everyone's off on holiday, which is the way you like it. Now, you can get on with your stuff uninterrupted.

September – A good month for the Ox break. Of course you've got time (again). An unusual destination appeals.

October – Two admirers seem to want your attention, Ox. How do you choose?

November – Making your own gifts seems like fun. It's time to show off your crafty skills.

December – A big family get-together beckons. Good to see the whole Ox clan under one roof. Enjoy.

Lucky colours for 2025: Blue, Black, White

Lucky numbers for 2025: 1, 4

Three Takeaways

Lighten up

Relax

Make time for socialising

CHAPTER 11: THE TIGER

Tiger Years

13 February 1926 – 1 February 1927

31 January 1938 – 18 February 1939

17 February 1950 – 5 February 1951

5 February 1962 – 24 January 1963

23 January 1974 – 10 February 1975

9 February 1986 – 28 January 1987

28 January 1998 – 5 February 1999

14 February 2010 – 2 February 2011

1 February 2022 – 21 January 2023

19 February 2034 – 7 February 2035

6 February 2046 – 25 January 2047

Natural Element: Wood

Will 2025 be a Glorious Year for the Tiger?

Okay, Tiger, no doubt you're flicking through your new calendar, pencilling in some vital dates, and wondering just how 2025 is going to work out. Well, you'll be glad to know it's going to be another year to really get your teeth into.

2024, if you're typical of your sign, is likely to have been punctuated with some monumental rows. They were impossible to avoid because you and the Dragon ruler of the year are the biggest, fieriest beasts in the zodiac. You each think you're the boss and are quite prepared to trade blows to prove it.

Not that you're bothered, Tiger (any more than the Dragon is). Unlike some of the more delicate signs, you both find a vigorous and high-volume exchange of views immensely stimulating. You may pretend you don't enjoy the drama, but – in truth – you thrive on it.

So, the last year has probably been turbulent but pretty successful in the long run for most Tigers. Now, you can look forward to round two.

Yes, in some ways, 2025 is similar to 2024 in that it is another Wood year, and the Snake ruler is a great mate of the Dragon and quite prepared to continue some of Dragon's favourite themes.

Since you're a Wood creature – just like the Dragon – the bold, expansive energy of the year suited you and your projects well, despite a superficial clash here and there. You've got some of the same beneficial aspects going for you in 2025, Tiger, but with added complications thrown in, courtesy of the serpent.

For a start, the Snake is not one of your biggest fans, although the two of you don't clash like you and the Dragon. Snake doesn't do noisy battles, but the Snake's silent deviousness can make things difficult in ways that might take you by surprise. Then there's the fact that the Snake is a Fire creature. Fire likes Wood, of course (for obvious reasons), but Wood is not so comfortable around Fire. Wood signs can end up feeling exhausted or used when Fire is in charge.

So, how will this work out in everyday life, Tiger? Expansion in your career and your finances will continue in a pleasing way, plus a number of exciting opportunities will arrive out of the blue. These offers could really put you in the big time, so most Tigers will be eager to accept. Yet the Snake will make you fight for them – not physically – but with subtle mind games. You'll be required to sharpen your wits and devise complicated strategies if you're to win the prizes you want.

Yet once you realise what's going on, you'll relish the challenge. This situation is a bit different for the Tiger brain, and you can't resist the intriguing novelty. And, of course, you always play to win so life could get intense.

The other thing about you, Tiger, is that you're a rebel at heart. The Dragon year will have got you fired up on a number of causes, and typical Tigers will now be ready to move forward and take action.

Protest marches could feature heavily on many Tiger to-do lists in 2025, while others may decide to move into politics or some similarly idealistic activism (albeit behind the scenes). Clever Snake is pointing out the benefits of pulling the strings silently, from an unnoticed position, but this approach is not easy for typical Tigers. A full frontal, head-on charge with the big cat in the lead is more your style.

Getting your head around this year's invisible power play could be irritating for you, Tiger. You don't want to be bothered with such convoluted nonsense, but you're aware that if you ignore it, you could end up being used. The best plan is to partner up in some way with one of the Snake's best buddies. A comrade born under the sign of the Ox, Rooster, Monkey, or even the Dragon (if you don't mind a few rows) could help you negotiate the Snake's wiles with ease.

You usually prefer to go it alone, Tiger, but this year, if you join forces with a favoured ally, you'll be unbeatable.

The Wonder of Being a Tiger

How could it not be wonderful to be a Tiger? Big, bold, and beautiful, with a strong, athletic body, proud swagger and uncompromisingly individual style that manages to be magnificent yet strangely wild. People notice you, Tiger, and their jaws tend to drop. There is an awe-inspiring quality about you that they can't quite explain.

In China, the sign of the Tiger is regarded as fortunate and noble. The Tiger can't help but be a symbol of good fortune, of course, since in any jungle battle, the big cat is bound to come out on top. But the Chinese also emphasise a nobility about this sign.

Zodiac Tigers are fearless. They will fight with enormous courage, but their clashes are seldom for personal gain. Typical Tiger is prepared to battle to the death for a just cause, an abused underdog, or to defeat a tyrannical authority. The Tiger is a born revolutionary.

People born under this sign have been known to lose every penny they possess in the resulting struggle, but they don't really care. They're not materialistic. Money in the bank or frivolous knick-knacks mean little to them. If they have to sacrifice such trivialities for a good cause, it's worth it.

Yet the Chinese also believe the Tiger's stupendous, two-tone coat – the flaming orange, slashed with vivid stripes of darkest black – indicates a nature that has two sides.

Zodiac Tigers, while quite prepared to risk everything to aid a stranger in need, can turn surprisingly unsympathetic to close friends or relatives who've behaved foolishly.

What's more, the Tiger has an unpredictable temper and can change from purring pussy cat to snarling carnivore in an instant. Other signs tend to recognise this instinctively, and few will risk upsetting the big cat on purpose. Only the boldest Dragon or strongest Ox will dare tweak the Tiger's tail now and then.

Despite this, most Tigers are popular and charming. Their glamour and strength draws admirers to them, and – when things are going well – their inner kitten delights all companions. They know they can be a tad scary, so they keep their claws sheathed the majority of the time and collect a wide circle of loyal followers as a result.

Yet, somehow, and at some level, the Tiger always walks alone. Just as the Tiger doesn't really mind whether they have material goods or not, the big cat is also not fussed about having a companion along.

Tigers are great travellers; they're restless souls who hate to be in the same place for too long. So, the typical Tiger is always finding an excuse for another trip. Home or abroad, the Tiger doesn't mind just as long as they're on the move, although far-flung places do hold a special appeal to the big cat's imagination. And if a mate fancies joining Tiger on the Tiger's travels, that's fine; if not, the Tiger is just as happy to go alone.

This is a sign that scoffs at caution. Tigers take risks… every day. And the annoying thing, as far as their more wary zodiac cousins are concerned, is that the Tiger invariably escapes unscathed from situations where other signs would come severely unstuck. There's no doubt you're a lucky sign, Tiger, just don't forget cats only have nine lives.

The Tiger Home

Probably the most important item in the Tiger home is the Tiger passport. Followed by the Tiger suitcase, rucksack, and overnight bag.

The other thing about the Tiger abode, which visitors probably wouldn't notice at first, is that there's a handy escape route nearby. Easy access to a car, bus stop, or train station, plus an unobstructed front door, is essential. People born under this sign have to feel free.

Beyond that, the Tiger home is likely to be airy and furnished with clean lines and pale colours. Large windows and (where possible) bifold doors admit maximum light, and paintings and posters of greenery and outdoor scenes brighten the walls. The typical Tiger likes growing things but doesn't bother with houseplants unless there's someone to water them while Tiger's away. The same goes for pets.

The typical Tiger isn't much interested in housework or cooking either, so the kitchen is little used and the fridge bare, but there's a dishwasher if possible. Tiger does invite the occasional guest now and then and entertains them with takeaway meals and generous glasses of the latest exotic brew brought back from Tiger's travels. Somehow, it all hangs together, and visitors are happy to return.

Being Friends with the Tiger

It's not always easy being friends with the Tiger. Magnetic and original, the Tiger attracts admirers and people feel rather privileged to be admitted to the big cat's inner circle. What's more, as a Tiger friend, you'll never be bored; lively Tiger has an endless stream of entertaining tales and extraordinary info picked up on their trips. Plus, the Tiger has always got a project or an exciting new place to explore lined up and friends are welcome to get involved. The Tiger's not at all clingy and expects little from you in return.

Yet, the Tiger can be moody. One day, they're the sunniest of souls; the next grouchy and uncommunicative. They always seem to be falling out with someone, too, for reasons that are unclear. And then, just as you're beginning to get to know them better, they're going away again and they're not sure when they'll be back.

So, it's great to be friends with a Tiger as long as you don't need a shoulder to lean on or a regular companion for your own interests.

Tiger Superpowers

Stunning presence

Fearless

Devotion to justice

Best Jobs for Tiger in 2025

Environmental Activist

Social Worker

Detective

Insurance Investigator

Politician

Overseas Aid Worker

Perfect Partners

Cupid's arrow can strike anywhere at any time, of course, but once the novelty of new romance wears off, some relationships are easier to maintain than others. Here's a guide to the Tiger's compatibility with other signs.

Tiger with Tiger

The attraction between these two beautiful people is powerful. They understand each other so well; it's almost like looking in a mirror. They both like to walk on the wild side and will enjoy some exciting adventures together, but their moody interludes could lead to fierce quarrels. This match could be compulsive but stormy.

Tiger with Rabbit

Surprisingly, the Rabbit is not intimidated by Tiger's dangerous aura, and this attitude immediately appeals to Tiger, who enjoys a challenge. Rabbit's calm presence and clever way with words keeps Tiger interested, while Rabbit finds Tiger's adventurous tales entertaining. With care, these two could get on well together for years.

Tiger with Dragon

The two biggest personalities in the zodiac would seem bound to clash. After all, these larger-than-life characters share so many similarities there's a danger they'd compete. Yet a relationship between the Tiger and Dragon often works very well. They understand each other's impulsive natures, but they're also different enough to supply the support the other needs. They'd make a formidable power couple.

Tiger with Snake

Not the best of romances. These two are so fundamentally different that any initial attraction is unlikely to last. Snake likes to bask and conserve energy, while Tiger wants to leap right in and race about. Tiger takes in the big picture in a glance and is off to the next challenge, while Snake likes to pause, delve beneath the surface, and consider. It wouldn't take long before these two annoy each other.

Tiger with Horse

This athletic pair get on pretty well. They both like physical pursuits, testing their strength out of doors or just enjoying the feel of the wind in their hair and the ground under their feet. True, Horse may not quite understand Tiger's plans for world domination, but it doesn't really matter. Horse is happy to be loyal to such a charismatic partner. As they're both moody, there could be rows, but making up is exciting.

Tiger with Goat

Tiger and Goat don't have a lot in common. While their aims and temperaments are quite different, they are both sociable creatures, and Goat wouldn't mind Tiger attracting all the attention when they're out together. Tiger, in return, would appreciate Goat's lack of jealousy and generosity of spirit. Yet, in the long term, they're likely to drift apart as they follow their different interests.

Tiger with Monkey

Tiger can't help being intrigued by sparkling Monkey, and Monkey is flattered by such interest. Who wouldn't enjoy being admired by such a fabulous creature? But irrepressible Monkey just can't help teasing, and being teased is not a sensation Tiger is familiar with nor appreciates. Unless the attraction is very strong, these two will wind each other up until they can bear it no longer and part.

Tiger with Rooster

The only feathered creature in the zodiac, the opulence and novelty of Rooster's appearance will draw Tiger like a magnet. What's more, deep down, they are both quite serious-minded types, so – on one level – they'll have much to share. Yet, despite this, they're not really on the same wavelength, and misunderstandings will keep recurring. Could be hard work.

Tiger with Dog

While not exactly opposites, these two are different enough to intrigue each other yet similar enough in basic outlook to get on well. Both Tiger and Dog are idealistic and uninterested in material gain, yet where Dog can be nervous, Tiger is bold; and where Tiger attracts controversy, Dog will be loyal. This partnership could be lasting and valuable.

Tiger with Pig

Carefree Pig will love to bask in Tiger's impressive aura, while Tiger will feel good about protecting this charming but unworldly creature. They enjoy each other's company and Tiger, so focused on lofty matters, will find Pig's compulsive shopping too trivial to worry about. This couple could do well together as long as Pig's fondness for cosy nights in doesn't make Tiger feel trapped.

Tiger with Rat

Sleek and clever Rat can easily attract Tiger's attention because the intelligent Tiger loves witty conversation. Yet, these two are not natural partners. Tiger's not interested in Rat's latest bargain and has no wish to talk about it while Rat doesn't share Tiger's passion for changing the world. Still, if they can agree to step back and not get in each other's way, they could reach a good understanding.

Tiger with Ox

Not an easy match. Ox and Tiger could be on different planets. Fiery Tiger doesn't frighten Ox, and Tiger may admire Ox's strong, good looks and sincere nature, but they both need different things from life. Tiger wants to dash about creating big changes, while Ox reckons you get more done by buckling down where you happen to be and attending to the details. Clashes could abound.

Tiger Love 2025 Style

Okay let's face it, Tiger, the other signs are jealous of you. You're completely stunning, with totally natural good looks; that feline grace, that confident smile, that shining hair that falls into perfect place the second you turn your head – no other sign compares. Then there's the way you emphasise it all with a casually thrown-together look that manages to be both cutting edge and original, yet which you claim is purely accidental.

If you weren't surrounded by admirers the whole time, your rivals could get nasty. What gets their teeth really gnashing is your air of not even caring whether a partner materialises or not. This is doubly unfair, considering you clearly have your choice at any given moment.

Yet the point is, the single Tiger is being honest. While enjoying all the advantages and genuinely believing they're looking for a soulmate, other issues keep stealing their attention and they're usually too busy to pursue romance.

It's likely to happen again this year, single Tiger. A number of mouthwatering potential loves will enter your orbit, and you'll give them a whirl for a while. But then the lure of overseas will come calling and you're off. An intriguing foreigner could be your best bet in 2025.

Attached Tigers can look forward to a roller coaster year. Stand by for some epic rows, courtesy of the Snake, possibly caused by jealousy. Not so much the envy directed towards the single Tiger, but the jealousy of a partner who feels overlooked or cheated upon. You're not normally a cheat, Tiger, so if it's lack of attention that's upsetting them, it's time to make amends.

Secrets of Success in 2025

Success is yours this year, Tiger, if you're prepared to play by the serpent rules. This is awkward because you've never seen a rule you didn't want to break, and the Snake rules are particularly annoying to energetic 'doers' such as yourself.

Nevertheless, if you're prepared to compromise, you could shoot straight to the top. The Snake is demanding you slow down in 2025; calm that restless spirit and spend more time seated (possibly at a desk) but at any rate concentrating on the task at hand. You should also cut down on some of those trips. We all know most of them aren't really business, so it's no good pretending.

You have great potential, Tiger, but you tend to scatter your energies and fail to achieve as highly as you could. This year, if you choose one main project, devote most of your time to it and put the other items, including travel, on the back burner until it's complete, you could end up with a success that's absolutely stunning. Linking up with one of those other signs previously mentioned – Ox, Rooster, Monkey or Dragon – could give you the extra impetus you need.

Just be on the alert for certain members in the family circle acting unreasonably and throwing you off course. Bad tempers are expanding under the influence of Wood. Don't engage, or you risk starting a blaze that will be difficult to put out.

The Tiger Year at a Glance

January – Dull, dull, dull. Is it too early for skiing?

February – Things are looking up. An intriguing offer arrives in your inbox.

March – A new recruit at work wants your advice. You're busy but kinda flattered. How can you refuse?

April – An old rival reappears on the scene. You know just how to handle them.

May – You're planning your travels, but someone disagrees. Should you please them or go it alone?

June – A crazy friend signs you up for a protest demo. Looks like a good cause.

July – An elderly relative wants to drag you on a trip. You're not keen, but your kind heart prevails.

August – An attractive stranger is eyeing you up. You're way too busy to get involved. But on the other hand…

September – That restless streak is getting stronger. Time to get the passport out.

October – Another protest is on the cards. You so enjoyed the first one. Could you join the cause professionally?

November – Someone you met abroad is back here and wants to meet up. Could be fun.

December – Somehow, you're double- and possibly triple-booked for the festivities. Oops. Some fast talking is required.

Lucky colours for 2025: Red, Orange, Gold

Lucky numbers for 2025: 3, 1

Three Takeaways

Stay calm
Recruit an ally
Focus

CHAPTER 12: THE RABBIT

Rabbit Years

2 February 1927 – 22 January 1928

19 February 1939 – 7 February 1940

6 February 1951 – 26 January 1952

25 January 1963 – 12 February 1964

11 February 1975 – 30 January 1976

29 January 1987 – 16 February 1988

6 February 1999 – 4 February 2000

3 February 2011 – 22 January 2012

22 January 2023 – 9 February 2024

8 February 2035 – 27 January 2036

26 January 2047 – 13 February 2048

Natural Element: Wood

Will 2025 be a Glorious Year for the Rabbit?

Annnnd relax… Good news, Rabbit. At long last, you can sit back, put your feet up, and take it easy. It's been over 12 months now since you were ruler of the year – back in 2023 – yet you've not been able to enjoy the release from authority quite as much as you hoped.

It all looked so promising at the changeover. There was the Dragon of 2024 eager to take the reins from you and quite prepared to help you get settled into your low-key new groove. Yet, if you're typical of your sign,

Rabbit, it didn't quite work out that way. The trouble is the Dragon means well, but Dragon's idea of low-key is quite unlike that of most other signs and not remotely like yours.

Consequently, many Rabbits found themselves buffeted along, responding to opportunities and lucrative offers that were highly positive but overwhelming in the speed and frequency of their arrival.

Then, there was the possibility of changes at home and in the family circle, which while not necessarily bad, were nevertheless unsettling to the orderly Rabbit sensibilities.

Blame it all on the combination of the exceptionally dynamic Dragon combined with the Wood energy of the year. The entire thrust of 2024 was devoted to the expansion and growth of everything, and at the highest possible speed. Exhilarating for the toughest signs but exhausting for gentler types such as you.

Happily, Rabbit, things couldn't go on like that forever. And now the soothing Snake has arrived to bring a little more serenity to the proceedings. Don't get carried away with applause, though, Rabbit.

This is another Wood year, and the Snake is a great mate of the Dragon, so there's a similar feel in the air and the Snake is prepared to continue with some of Dragon's enthusiasms.

Yet the Wood energy of 2025 is a much softer, slower, more tranquil version than last year's hurricane force. Far more to your taste, Rabbit. What's more, you're a Wood creature yourself, so the atmosphere in its quieter form suits you very well.

At last, you can slow down and make the progress you want at your own pace for a change. Business Rabbits will be delighted to find that new clients, new outlets, and new projects are gradually snowballing and developing successfully. Employed Rabbits are more appreciated than ever. You're likely to be asked to take on more responsibility and – as your expertise is recognised – many employed Rabbits will be encouraged to get involved in training new staff.

Cash is no problem this year as the Wood element sends it rolling into the Rabbit coffers. It may come in the form of a salary increase along with that promotion, it may be the spoils of that booming business, or it may even be the result of an unexpected win, but somehow a boost to the Rabbit finances will find its way to you. Many a Rabbit will be inspired to splash the cash on a fabulous family holiday or some long-awaited home renovations – which, of course, puts a big smile on the faces of the Rabbit clan.

If there's any friction set to disturb the Rabbit peace, it's likely to be down to the fact that Snake is a Fire creature and Rabbit is Wood. While

Fire approves of Wood and seeks it out, for obvious reasons, when the two get together too closely, Wood has a nasty habit of going up in flames. In day-to-day life, this could play out as an unwise venture going expensively wrong, or an abrasive person attempting to make trouble in the Rabbit circle.

You can cope with it, Rabbit, so don't worry. You may be sensitive, but you're extremely capable.

Rabbits are also likely to be affected by a couple of the Snake's other unique characteristics. The Snake is a mysterious, mystic sign known for creating strange vibes in certain quarters. Many a down-to-earth Rabbit could be baffled to find themselves unaccountably drawn to the uncanny side of life this year, with intriguing results.

Plus, of course, the Snake is also famous for sudden, unexpected moves. Chances are, a big surprise is brewing behind the scenes for you, Rabbit. You'll never guess, but when all is revealed, you'll love it.

The Wonder of Being a Rabbit

Star of many an Easter card and welcome emblem of Spring, the gentle Rabbit offends no one – unless you happen to be a market gardener, of course.

Basically, everyone loves the cuddly bunny; so harmless a creature it's regarded as the perfect toy for the tiniest baby. The Chinese associate the zodiac Rabbit with good luck as well as peace and harmony. The most admirable of qualities.

Yet don't be fooled by that softest of soft fur and the cute little powder puff bobtail. The Rabbit may come over as timid and vulnerable, but in fact it's a great survivor. Wherever Rabbits thrive, there are tireless predators, yet the defenceless Rabbit mostly evades them all and manages to hop on, multiplying regardless. Along with the Rat, the Rabbit is an incredibly successful species.

People often underestimate you, Rabbit, with your soft voice, quiet appearance, and perfect manners – yet you are much tougher than you look. And, of course, if you're typical of your sign, Rabbit, you usually find this quite useful. Rivals tend to let their guard down around the unthreatening Rabbit – a mistake from which clever Rabbit unobtrusively benefits.

Vulgarity is almost physically painful to the true bobtail. Rabbits are instinctively classy with cultured tastes. They love art, restraint in all things, and order. Messy surroundings, eye-searingly clashing colours, loud noises, and pungent smells make them feel ill. Raised voices and torrid quarrels, meanwhile, can bring on a migraine.

No wonder the sensitive Rabbit strives for harmony above all else. People born under this sign are the peacemakers of the universe. They have a knack for persuading the most bitter of enemies to agree to compromise. They refuse to take sides, see everyone's point of view, quell discord, and somehow wind up friends with all parties.

Rabbits are such born diplomats they really should consider applying to the government for a professional role. No one has to teach Rabbit to be tactful or discreet. These qualities are written through the bobtails, like the letters through a stick of rock.

What's more, the typical Rabbit always finds the perfect words for every occasion. They're never pushy but they know just what to say to nudge situations the way they want them to go. They are such brilliant strategists – possibly because the bunny, having no physical means to defend itself, is forced to get by on wits alone. For this reason, people born under this sign usually rise to the top of whatever profession they happen to have chosen, leaving their colleagues scratching their heads as to how they achieved it.

Yet, as satisfying as career success may be, the true Rabbit's real passion is family. Family comes first as far as Rabbit is concerned, and if all is well with the loved ones, Rabbit is content.

The Rabbit Home

You're in for a treat if you get invited to the Rabbit home. Only the most favoured guests are wafted across the Rabbit threshold because the bobtail warren is a precious sanctuary. But should you be trusted enough to get inside, you'll find a beautifully decorated, softly lit space with a wonderfully soothing atmosphere. Harmonious colours (naturally) blend perfectly into each other, the walls resemble an art gallery, and tasteful objects are displayed in just the right places to catch the eye but not jar. There are often quite a few children in residence, yet somehow the place remains miraculously tidy. The Rabbit is a wonderful host and guests are spoiled with dainty nibbles and the finest beverages, while the bobtail children tumble about delighting everyone with their innocent charm. You can't wait to go back.

Being Friends with the Rabbit

Since the Rabbit gets on with everyone, it's more difficult not to be friends with the Rabbit. Yet there are friends, and then there are *real* friends. Rabbit probably doesn't realise it, but most of the Rabbit friends could more properly be classed as friendly acquaintances. Rabbit has dozens of these: workmates, business associates, neighbours, and people

Rabbit met on the school run. Yet the *real* friends tend to be small in number and have known Rabbit for years. These are the people Rabbit feels completely at ease with and is happy to see at any time. They probably met at school or university and have shared all life's ups and downs ever since. But whichever category you fall into, the point is that Rabbit will never annoy you and should you annoy the Rabbit, you'll likely never find out. Reduce the chances of this, if possible, by removing your shoes on entering the Rabbit abode, refraining from all criticism, never speaking in harsh tones and – above all – avoiding arguments with any of Rabbit's guests. Keep to these rules, and you'll never be crossed off Rabbit's Christmas card list.

Rabbit Superpowers

Supreme tact

Discretion

Perfect taste

Best Jobs for Rabbits 2025

Garden Designer

Wedding Cake Maker

Party Planner

Art Gallery Worker

Psychiatrist

GP Receptionist

Perfect Partners

Cupid's arrow can strike anywhere at any time, of course, but once the novelty of new romance wears off, some relationships are easier to maintain than others. Here's a guide to the Rabbit's compatibility with other signs.

Rabbit with Rabbit

These two gorgeous creatures look like they're made for each other. Their relationship will always be calm, peaceful, and unruffled, and it goes without saying that their home could grace a glossy magazine. Yet, though they never argue, the willingness of both partners to compromise could end up with neither ever quite doing what they want. Ultimately, they may find the spark goes out.

Rabbit with Dragon

Dragon is such a larger-than-life character, Rabbit could feel overwhelmed at times. Also, the Dragon can be rather noisy and overdramatic, which would get on Rabbit's nerves. Yet they each admire the other's good points. If they could live next door to each other instead of under the same roof, a long-term relationship might work.

Rabbit with Snake

This subtle pair could make a good combination. They both understand the value of working behind the scenes, and neither has any desire to wear themselves out on endless adventures. They share a love of art, fine things, and quiet pleasures, and they both enjoy an orderly home. These two could settle down very happily together.

Rabbit with Horse

This could be tricky. It's fairly unlikely that Horse and Rabbit would ever end up on a date, but if they did, and there was a strong attraction, it could lead to a love/hate relationship. Rabbit's neat and tidy ways would enrage Horse, and Horse's unpredictable moods and over-the-top reactions would annoy Rabbit. Soon, Horse is likely to bolt for the hills or Rabbit retreat to its burrow.

Rabbit with Goat

Happy-go-lucky Goat is very appealing to Rabbit, particularly as deep-down Rabbit is a bit of a worrier. They're both sociable without needing to be the centre of attention and would be happy to people-watch for hours and then cheerfully compare notes afterwards. Goat is tolerant of Rabbit's need for some regular alone time to recharge, too, so this couple could be a successful match.

Rabbit with Monkey

Mercurial Monkey doesn't really 'get' Rabbit. The Monkey can appreciate how well Rabbit operates and sees this approach gets good results, but it's all too picky and slow for Monkey. Rabbit, on the other hand, is amused by Monkey's quick wit and clever ways but deplores Monkey's slapdash, sometimes devious tactics. Very unlikely to work out.

Rabbit with Rooster

Another difficult match. However unfair it seems, Rooster comes over as loud, boastful, and uncouth to Rabbit, while Rabbit appears dull, staid, and insufficiently admiring of Rooster's fine feathers to appeal to Rooster. These two just can't see below the surface of the other, and it would be surprising if they ended up together. Only to be considered by the very determined.

Rabbit with Dog

Despite the fact that in the outside world, Rabbit could easily end up as Dog's dinner, the astrological pair get on surprisingly well. Dog appreciates Rabbit's careful, efficient ways and soft voice, while Rabbit admires Dog's energy and good intentions. Dog's lack of interest in the finer points of interior design might try Rabbit's patience, but with a little work, these two could reach an understanding.

Rabbit with Pig

Pig is not quite as interested in fine dining as Rabbit, being as happy to scoff a burger as a Cordon Bleu creation, but their shared love of the good things in life makes these two happy companions. Once again, Pig's spending habits might irritate Rabbit, but not too much, as Rabbit is quite willing to splurge on lovely things for the home. A relationship would work well.

Rabbit with Rat

Rat finds Rabbit intriguing. Here is an attractive, stylish creature that doesn't feel the need to be pushy or take centre stage yet somehow manages to be at the heart of things, while Rabbit is flattered and entertained by witty Rat's attention. These two respect each other but, in the long term, Rat could be too overpowering unless they both agree to give each other space.

Rabbit with Ox

Ox finds Rabbit rather cute and appealing. Whether male or female, there's something about Rabbit's inner fluffiness that brings out Ox's highly developed protective instincts. Rabbit, meanwhile, loves the Ox's reassuring presence and the sense of security Ox provides. These two could get on very well together as long as refined Rabbit can overlook Ox's occasional down-to-earth – Rabbit might say 'coarse' – observations.

Rabbit with Tiger

Surprisingly, the Rabbit is not intimidated by Tiger's dangerous aura, and this attitude immediately appeals to Tiger, who enjoys a challenge. Rabbit's calm presence and clever way with words keeps Tiger interested, while Rabbit finds Tiger's adventurous tales entertaining. With care, these two could get on well together for years.

Rabbit Love 2025 Style

If you're not a model Rabbit, you could certainly be mistaken for one. You glide into a room, not necessarily conventionally good-looking but so perfectly, elegantly put together that all eyes turn your way as you float gracefully to a quiet corner.

You may hope to relax there unobtrusively, Rabbit, but there's no chance of that. You exude such a fascinating aura that other signs keep glancing over for a second, third, or even a fourth look.

Yet, even though you're not in any way hostile or unfriendly, few dare to come over to make your acquaintance. You're just too lovely. They suspect you're out of their league.

Fortunately, the single Rabbit knows exactly what to do. Single Rabbit has a mysterious way of meandering serenely to the edge of whatever group contains a sign of interest and hovering there, until by some invisible magic, that person detaches themself and moves off with Rabbit.

No one knows how you do it, Rabbit, but you're doing it again this year with even more success than usual. Despite your gentle looks, you can be a bit of a heartbreaker, though. You may audition quite a few admirers, but you're picky about the ones you decide to keep. Nonetheless, you let them go so tactfully it's often weeks before they realise it's over. Be kind this year, Rabbit.

Attached Rabbits may find their beloved acting a little mysteriously in 2025. Something is going on, and you suspect they have a plan for you. You're right. They do. Looks like it's going to be fun, though. Wait and see.

Secrets of Success in 2025

Phew. Hopefully, you've got your breath back now, Rabbit. If you're typical of your sign, you were rushed off your feet last year.

Luckily, 2025 will be much easier for you. The Snake appreciates that high speed is rarely necessary, and there's no need to make a drama out of every hitch. You can slow down and take your time, calmly considering each move with a clear conscience. The Snake has your back.

Yet, this energy does come with its own hazards. In Snake years, things are rarely as simple as they appear. There are hidden layers upon layers. Deception and untruths tend to flourish in dark corners, and it's quite possible you'll encounter at least one rogue or scammer who tries to trick you. You may also discover that someone in your circle has been economical with the truth, to put it mildly.

No need to panic, but think carefully before taking any risks and check out all new faces with extra diligence.

The Rabbit Year at a Glance

January – A relative could do with a helping hand. They don't like to ask, so watch them carefully.

February – Authority figures are taking an interest in you. You have some expertise they could use. Play your cards right, Rabbit.

March – All becomes clear. The boss lays it out. More work, more responsibility. More money, too?

April – A family drama blows up. Good thing you're so diplomatic, Rabbit. Think oil on troubled waters.

May – Someone in your circle has been caught out exaggerating. Or is it fantasising? Can you spare their feelings?

June – A work colleague wants extra holiday. Or at least the dates other people bagged. Down to you to intervene.

July – Romance is in the air. An arty break is proposed but can you spare the time? Of course, Rabbit.

August – A big family get-together or joint holiday trip comes around. Good to catch up with all the old faces.

September – A new boss or a new neighbour starts throwing their weight about. They think you're a pushover, Rabbit. Show them how wrong they can be!

October – Your bank balance gets a boost. Big celebrations all around.

November – The festive season's racing towards you. There are a lot of little bunnies to buy for. Happy shopping.

December – Busy socialising before the holidays. You're glad to enjoy a quieter Christmas with the family.

Lucky colours for 2025: Purple, Turquoise, Mint

Lucky numbers for 2025: 3, 4, 9

Three Takeaways

Be alert for scammers
Concentrate on trusted faces
Spend wisely

CHAPTER 13: THE DRAGON

Dragon Years

23 January 1928 – 9 February 1929

8 February 1940 – 26 January 1941

27 January 1952 – 13 February 1953

13 February 1964 – 1 February 1965

31 January 1976 – 17 February 1977

17 February 1988 – 5 February 1989

5 February 2000 – 23 January 2001

23 January 2012 – 9 February 2013

10 February 2024 – 28 January 2025

28 January 2036 – 14 February 2037

Natural Element: Wood

Will 2025 be a Glorious Year for the Dragon?

Congratulations, Dragon. Come on, come to the front of the stage, and take a bow. We know you're not shy. Soak up that well-deserved applause and have a last bask in the spotlight. Okay, so there might be a few boos, too, but you can ignore them. You can't please everyone.

You've successfully completed your first year in charge since 2012 (well, to be precise, since the Wood Dragon of 1964). And what a year it's been, Dragon. Dramatic, energising, progressive. Alright, so maybe there were some negative events along the way, but no one's perfect.

The point is few people will forget 2024 in a hurry. You've made your mark.

Now, it's time to head for the wings and leave the stage to your good mate, the Snake.

Though you love the attention, Dragon, and if you're typical of your sign, you're probably not as sorry as you expected to hand over your crown.

Everyone thinks they want to run the show and, of course, it's enormous fun to begin with. You can get a bit drunk with power. But when the reality sets in, you realise the job comes with enormous responsibility. You get blamed for everything that goes wrong. You're forced to make decisions when, in truth, you can't make up your mind. Some things don't work out as you planned. It ends up more of a learning curve, sometimes painfully so, than an excuse to let your hair down, boss everyone about, and enjoy yourself.

So, that's why you're actually much more likely to have a blast in 2025 than you were last year. There's a wonderful sense of pressure being released. You didn't realise you were getting tired but – now you've stopped – you're thrilled to be able to slow down and relax. Well, just a little, Dragon. The Dragon's idea of relaxation is quite different to that of most other signs.

Even better is the fact that you're handing over to the Snake. The Snake is a good friend and admires your genius, Dragon. Snake wants to help you make the most of your talents. Plus, this is another Wood year (like last year), and you are a Wood creature, so beneficial energy surrounds you on every level. True, the Snake happens to belong to the Fire tribe and being around too much fire tends to make Wood creatures nervous. In your case, though, you're so strong and powerful – compared with this little flame – it merely adds a pleasurable frisson of excitement.

If you're typical of your sign, Dragon, you will have enjoyed many good things last year, but that's nothing compared with the luck that's in store in 2025. Projects begun in 2024 properly bear fruit in the coming months and people are beginning to take notice. It looks like you're making a name for yourself, Dragon. You could even end up famous in your field.

Without realising it, it seems many a Dragon planted numerous seeds last year, and suddenly they're all germinating. The typical Dragon was in an expansive mood and decided to experiment with a variety of new activities and projects. Who knew you could have so many talents, Dragon?

You might have believed you were only playing around to see what would happen, but now your new skills are developing well and gaining momentum. As a result, many Dragons will be presented with unusual new career opportunities this year.

Employed Dragons have become the boss's favourite pet, while rival companies try to poach them away. It's good to be popular, Dragon. Business Dragons find they're branching out in all kinds of exciting directions, while artistic and student Dragons score success after success, arousing jealousy in less fortunate signs.

If that wasn't enough, Dragon, you don't need to worry about finances this year. Your previous efforts are turning to gold and it's flowing straight into the Dragon hoard, soon to be followed by the cash generated by your new projects. You're not a materialistic sign, but you love the freedom of choice this gives you.

Last year, many a Dragon welcomed new faces into the family and also changed their home. Those that didn't quite finalise the move will be aided by the Snake this year. Even those Dragons with no intention of uprooting may find themselves involved in a new property of some kind. Shepherd's hut in a meadow anyone? Caravan by the sea? However it pans out, it looks like you'll be out and about much more this year, Dragon. Time to spread those enormous wings.

The Wonder of Being a Dragon

You really are quite annoying, Dragon. No wonder the other signs are secretly envious of you. You might think that being the only mythical creature in the zodiac was a disadvantage, but no, you've got it all.

Good looks, charm, strength, talent, energy. Plus, of course, the Chinese regard you as the luckiest sign of the lot, not only enjoying a fortunate life yourself but also bringing good luck to the family in which you were born.

No wonder the birth rate in Chinese communities rises noticeably in a Dragon year. Everyone wants a Dragon baby if it's physically possible.

The typical Dragon is enthusiastic, extroverted, totally honest, and incredibly energetic. In fact, you're a bit overpowering for some of the more low-key signs, Dragon. In true Dragon style, though, you probably don't even notice.

Dragons mean well. They have so many gifts they take their good fortune for granted. Full of optimism and creativity and buzzing with ideas, they dash about enlisting support for their latest project – and getting it – without even realising they've not finished the last.

Point this out, and Dragon's likely to shrug good-naturedly and assure everyone that everything's in hand.

These people think BIG and have a gift for inspiring others, but they get bored easily and quickly move on to the next adventure when the previous one gets tedious.

The typical Dragon is a bit of a star and usually rises to the top of whatever workplace they find themselves in. They make excellent leaders, but only if they have a good number two at their side. A Snake, for instance. This is because while the Dragon excels at the big picture, the all-important picky details tend to make their eyes glaze over. They really can't be bothered, and this trait often gets them into trouble.

Yet the Dragon is seldom without cash for long – despite the risks they can't help taking. Their obvious gifts attract money and they frequently end up wealthy. Bafflingly to other signs, though, the typical Dragon is not particularly interested in an overflowing bank account and is not motivated by money – though they will accept any contributions offered.

No, what gets the Dragon up in the morning is a new goal, a tempting adventure, or just being in on the action. A Dragon without a cause, a plan, or an idea to explore is a very depressed Dragon indeed.

Dragons are friendly and kind-hearted and can be suckers for a hard luck story. They'll give generously to someone in need and can be relied on to do the right thing, even if it's against their own interests. Yet they get so carried away with their own enthralling plans they can be surprisingly insensitive to the people around them.

But what other signs don't realise is that for all its confidence, the Dragon is easily hurt. Reject the Dragon, and Dragon will withdraw for days, deeply wounded, although too proud to admit it. What a complicated sign you are, Dragon.

The Dragon Home

The public rooms in the Dragon home are likely to be light, airy, and feature very large windows. Dragons like to be able to see as much sky as possible. Should the property also overlook water, Dragon is unlikely ever to move. Yet few visitors get to admire the Dragon abode since most Dragons are far too busy for mundane tasks such as housework. They tend to acquire so much 'stuff' in connection with their latest project that the majority of surfaces are covered with brochures, papers, and sundry pieces of equipment. There isn't really room for guests. Dragon would much rather meet friends and relatives in the nearest pub or coffee shop. The few guests that get past the door will receive a warm welcome, however, as long as they don't mind clearing a space for themselves on the nearest sofa and making their own cup of coffee in the kitchen. Probably making one for Dragon while they're at it, too. What no one will see (except the closest of relatives) is the dim little room hidden away at the back: the Dragon lair. Stuffed with soft cushions, places to sprawl, and thick curtains, this is where Dragon retreats when things get too much even for the mighty Dragon.

Being Friends with the Dragon

The Dragon loves friends and tends to collect quite a few, so it's easy to strike up a friendship with people from this sign. The trouble is they're so busy and have such an extensive network, they're likely to forget about you. They're such fun to be with and such stimulating company, however, you probably won't mind, but you'll have to be prepared to do all the running and make the effort to stay in touch. What's more, in any circle, the Dragon can't help ending up being the centre of attention. They don't intend to dominate, but somehow they just do. This is fine for most signs content to bask in Dragon's entertaining glow. Yet others find this behaviour insufferable. Should you be a zodiac Tiger or Dog, you may find extrovert Dragon too much to take. And then there's the way the cheerful Dragon can suddenly turn morose and disappear alone for extended periods for no apparent reason. They'll never talk about it, but some slight or other thing has hurt their feelings. Leave them be, though, and after a while they'll bounce back as if nothing's happened.

Dragon Superpowers

Confidence

Enthusiasm

Creativity

Best Jobs for Dragon 2025

The Boss

Movie Star

Religious Leader

Composer

Auctioneer

Entrepreneur

Politician

Perfect Partners

Cupid's arrow can strike anywhere at any time, of course, but once the novelty of new romance wears off, some relationships are easier to maintain than others. Here's a guide to the Dragon's compatibility with other signs.

Dragon with Dragon

When Dragon meets Dragon, onlookers tend to take a step back and hold their breath. These two are a combustible mix – they either love each other or loathe each other. They are so alike, it could go either way. Both dazzling in their own orbits, they can't fail to notice the other's charms, but since they both need to be centre stage, things could get competitive. With give and take and understanding, this match could work well, but it won't be easy.

Dragon with Snake

Surprisingly, this couple gets along beautifully. Snake's elegant appearance and quick but subtle mind intrigues Dragon, while Snake admires Dragon's success and endless energy. Snake has no need to battle for the limelight and is quite happy to sit back and support Dragon's schemes from the comfort of a stylish sofa. Which is all the encouragement Dragon needs.

Dragon with Horse

The athletic Horse is pretty good at keeping up with dashing Dragon. And Dragon appreciates a partner who enjoys getting out and about as much as Dragon does. Yet Horse might grow weary of Dragon's constant new projects and resent having to be involved. Horse likes to go off and do Horsey things at frequent intervals which Dragon tends to view as disloyal. This relationship could get fiery.

Dragon with Goat

Goat tends to baffle the busy Dragon. Dragon can see Goat is the creative type but can't understand why Goat doesn't appear to be working very hard when so much could be achieved. In fact, if they stayed together long enough, Dragon could help Goat make the most of many talents, but it's unlikely either of them can sustain enough interest for this to happen.

Dragon with Monkey

These two are likely to hit it off immediately. Each is attracted to the other's intelligence and lively presence, and Dragon's exuberance doesn't overwhelm hyperactive Monkey. What's more, though they both enjoy being surrounded by a crowd, Monkey only wants to make people laugh, while Dragon hopes to inspire them to a cause. There is no conflict, so this couple can help each other to go far.

Dragon with Rooster

A Dragon and Rooster pairing will always attract attention. These two are both gorgeous beings and love to be surrounded by admirers. They will probably enjoy going out together and being seen as a couple, but in the long term, they may not be able to provide the kind of support each secretly needs.

Entertaining for a while, but probably not a lasting relationship.

Dragon with Dog

Not the easiest of combinations. Down-to-earth Dog can't see what all the fuss is about when it comes to Dragons. Unimpressed by glamour and irritated by what seems to Dog the gullibility of Dragon admirers, Dog can't be bothered to find out more. Dragon, meanwhile, is hurt by Dog's lack of interest. Great determination would be needed to make this work.

Dragon with Pig

While Dragon and Pig might seem to be opposites, the two of them can create a surprisingly contented relationship. Pig is quite happy for Dragon to fly around doing exciting things as long as Pig is not expected to do much more than admire profusely. Dragon appreciates Pig's uncritical support and makes allowances for Pig's lack of stamina. This couple could live in harmony.

Dragon with Rat

This couple is usually regarded as a very good match. They have much in common, being action-loving, excitement-seeking personalities who hate to be bored. It takes a lot to dazzle Rat, but the Dragon's glamorous aura proves irresistible, while Dragon loves to be admired, so each enjoys being with the other. There could be the odd power struggle as these two are both strong characters, but the magnetism is so intense they usually kiss and make up.

Dragon with Ox

Chalk and cheese, though this pair may appear to be, there's a certain fascination between them. Ox may not approve of Dragon's showy manner but recognises Dragon's good intentions, while Dragon admires Ox's strength of character and gift for completing tasks. If each could find a way to tolerate the other's wildly different lifestyles, they might be good for each other but, in the long term, Dragon's hectic pace might wear down even the Ox's legendary stamina.

Dragon with Tiger

The two biggest personalities in the zodiac would seem bound to clash. After all, these larger-than-life characters share so many similarities there's a danger they'd compete. Yet a relationship between the Tiger and Dragon often works well. They understand each other's impulsive natures, but they're also different enough to supply the support the other needs. They'd make a formidable power couple.

Dragon with Rabbit

Dragon is such a larger-than-life character, Rabbit could feel overwhelmed at times. Also, the Dragon can be rather noisy and overdramatic, which would get on Rabbit's nerves. Yet they each admire the other's good points. If they could live next door to each other instead of under the same roof, a long-term relationship might work.

Dragon Love 2025 Style

The Universe is organising a brilliant year of romance for you, Dragon – as it does every year in fact, though you may not even realise it. You have no idea that your success with admirers is not the normal state of affairs for most signs. You wander around, lit up like a movie star, when you've scarcely bothered to drag a comb through your hair. Should you decide to make an effort, you somehow emerge so stunning you end up stopping traffic.

It isn't like this for most people, Dragon!

This year, the sexy Snake is adding some additional fire to your allure, Dragon, and romance gets decidedly steamy. You're usually a bit 'take it or leave it' in your attitude to prospective partners, but now something's changed. A smouldering new alliance catches your attention and you keep going back for more. Just don't get burned, Dragon.

Attached Dragons are also aflame, courtesy of the fiery Snake. You and your beloved can suddenly find time for long candlelit nights at the Dragon abode, or for sneaking off for naughty weekends away. Make the most, Dragon.

Secrets of Success in 2025

You can't really go wrong this year, Dragon, if you just take it easy and let Snake do the heavy lifting. You prefer to be the boss, of course, so you're not keen on leaving things to others. Yet, this year, you can afford to coast in some areas and save your attention for certain important projects.

There's no need to run every show. Now, the Snake is encouraging you to concentrate on your creativity. Snake's Fire will fuel your imagination and the gentle Wood element of the year will coax your creations into growth. Do this, and by the time the Snake slides away, you should have a stack of new ventures up and running.

Just remember your unfortunate tendency to move on to the next interest before the previous one is complete. You give up too soon when you could have accomplished so much, Dragon. Stick to one thing at a time. Borrow some stamina from the Ox and complete what you start. Manage this, Dragon, and your prospects are dazzling.

The Dragon Year at a Glance

January – Admit it, you're a little fatigued, Dragon. A spa break could be just the tonic you need.

February – You're looking forward to Valetine's Day; more than one card is heading your way.

March – Renovations in the workplace. Maybe this is a good excuse to outsource? Check out new surroundings.

April – Someone in authority has big plans for you; your talents have been recognised. About time, Dragon.

May – Suddenly, you have an assistant – at home or at work. This helpful person could become indispensable.

June – Dragon energy is rising and you're wanted everywhere. Just the way you like it. You say yes to everything.

July – A craft-oriented friend takes you shopping. Not really your scene, Dragon, but you buy something to please them.

August – A project from the past gets revived and it's looking exciting. A few quick changes, and it's good to go.

September – A partner is demanding a holiday. Work is intriguing, but it's mean to refuse.

October – A new face in your circle seems a bit of a misery. Maybe they've got issues. Be kind, Dragon.

November – Cash is rolling in. You're good at saving, Dragon, but a property venture looks interesting.

December – Christmas dinner is being cooked for you, Dragon. They want to make a fuss of you. What a good idea! Don't protest. Enjoy!

Lucky colours for 2025: Black, Gold, Jade

Lucky numbers for 2025: 6, 8

Three Takeaways

Slow down
Stick to your plan
Don't forget to celebrate

CHAPTER 14: BUT THEN THERE'S SO MUCH MORE TO YOU

So now you know your animal sign, but possibly you're thinking – okay, but how can everyone born in the same year as me have the same personality as me?

You've only got to think back to your class at school, full of children the same age as you, to know this can't be true. And you're absolutely right. What's more, Chinese astrologers agree with you. For this reason, in Chinese astrology, your birth year is only the beginning. The month you were born and the hour of your birth are also ruled by the twelve zodiac animals – and not necessarily the same animal that rules your birth year.

These other animals then go on to modify the qualities of your basic year personality. So, someone born in an extrovert Tiger year but at the time of day ruled by the quieter Ox, and in the month of the softly spoken Snake, for instance, would very likely find their risk-taking Tiger qualities much toned down and enhanced by a few other calmer, more subtle traits.

By combining these three important influences, you get a much more accurate and detailed picture of the complex and unique person you really are. These calculations lead to so many permutations it soon becomes clear how people born in the same year can share various similarities, yet still remain quite different from each other.

What's more, the other animals linked to your date of birth can also have a bearing on how successful you will be in any year and how well you get on with people from other signs. Traditionally, the Horse and the Rabbit don't get on well together, for instance, so you'd expect two people born in these years to be unlikely to end up good friends. Yet if both individuals had other compatible signs in their charts, they could find themselves surprisingly warming to each other.

This is how it works:

Your Outer Animal – (Birth Year Creates Your First Impression)

You're probably completely unaware of it, but when people meet you for the first time, they will sense the qualities represented by the animal that ruled your birth year. Your Outer Animal and its personality influence the way you appear to the outside world. Your Outer animal is your public face. You may not feel the least bit like this creature deep down, and you may wonder why nobody seems to understand the real you. Why is it that people always seem to underestimate you, or perhaps overestimate you, you may ask yourself frequently. The reason is that you just can't help giving the impression of your birth-year animal and people will tend to see you and think of you in this way – especially if they themselves were born in other years.

Your Inner Animal – (Birth Month I The Private You)

Your Inner Animal is the animal that rules the month in which you were born. The personality of this creature tells you a lot about how you feel inside, what motivates you, and how you tend to live your life. When you're out in the world and want to present yourself in the best light, it's easy for you to project the finest talents of your birth-year animal. You've got them at your fingertips. But at home, with no one you need to impress, your Inner Animal comes to the fore. You can kick back and relax. You may find you have abilities and interests that no one at work would ever guess. Only your closest friends and loved ones are likely to get to know your Inner Animal.

By now you know your Outer Animal so you can move on to find your Inner Animal from the chart below:

Month of Birth - Your Inner Animal

January – the Ox

February – the Tiger

March – the Rabbit

April – the Dragon

May – the Snake

June – the Horse

July – the Goat

August – the Monkey

September – the Rooster

October – the Dog

November – the Pig

December – the Rat

Your Secret Animal – (Birth Hour I The Still, Small Voice Within)

Your secret animal rules the time you were born. Each 24-hour period is divided into 12, two-hour time-slots and each slot is believed to be ruled by a particular animal. This animal represents the deepest, most secret part of you. It's possibly the most intimate, individual part of you as it marks the moment you first entered the world and became 'you'. This animal is possibly your conscience and your inspiration. It might represent qualities you'd like to have or sometimes fail to live up to. Chances are, no one else will ever meet your Secret Animal.

For your Secret Animal check out the time of your birth:

Hours of Birth – Your Secret Animal

1 am – 3 am – the Ox

3 am – 5 am – the Tiger

5 am – 7 am – the Rabbit

7 am – 9 am – the Dragon

9 am – 11 am – the Snake

11 am – 1.00 pm – the Horse

1.00 pm – 3.00 pm – the Goat

3.00 pm – 5.00 pm – the Monkey

5.00 pm – 7.00 pm – the Rooster

7.00 pm – 9.00 pm – the Dog

9.00 pm – 11.00 pm – the Pig

11.00 pm – 1.00 am – the Rat

When you've found your other animals, go back to the previous chapters and read the sections on those particular signs. You may well discover talents and traits that you recognise immediately as belonging to you in addition to those mentioned in your birth year. It could also be that your Inner Animal or your Secret Animal is the same as your Year animal. A Dragon born at 8 am in the morning, for instance, will be a secret Dragon inside as well as outside, because the hours between 7 am and 9 am are ruled by the Dragon.

When this happens, it suggests that the positive and the less positive attributes of the Dragon will be held in harmony, so this particular Dragon ends up being very well balanced.

You might also like to look at your new animal's compatibility with other signs and see where you might be able to widen your circle of friends and improve your love life.

CHAPTER 15: IN YOUR ELEMENT

There's no doubt about it: Chinese astrology has many layers. But then we all recognise that we have many facets to our personalities, too. We are all more complicated than we might first appear. And more unique, as well.

It turns out that even people who share the same Chinese zodiac sign are not identical to people with the same sign but born in different years. A Snake born in 1965, for instance, will express their Snake personality in a slightly different way to a Snake born in 1977. This is not simply down to the influence of the other animals in their chart, it's because each year is also believed to be ruled by one of the five Chinese 'elements', as well as the year animal.

These elements are known as Water, Wood, Fire, Earth, and Metal.

Each element is thought to contain special qualities which are bestowed onto people born in the year it ruled, in addition to the qualities of their animal sign.

Since there are 12 signs endlessly rotating, and five elements, the same animal and element pairing only recurs once every 60 years. Which is why babies born in this 2025 Year of the Green Snake are unlikely to grow up remembering much about other Green Snakes from the previous generation. Those senior Green Snakes will already be 60 years old when the baby Green Snakes are born.

In years gone by, when life expectancy was lower, chances are there would only ever be one generation of a particular combined sign and element alive in the world at a time.

Find Your Element from the Chart Below:

The 1920s

5 February 1924 – 24 January 1925 | RAT | WOOD

25 January 1925 – 12 February 1926 | OX | WOOD

13 February 1926 – 1 February 1927 | TIGER | FIRE

2 February 1927 – 22 January 1928 | RABBIT | FIRE

23 January 1928 – 9 February 1929 | DRAGON | EARTH

10 February 1929 – 29 January 1930 | SNAKE | EARTH

The 1930s

30 January 1930 – 16 February 1931 | HORSE | METAL

17 February 1931 – 5 February 1932 | GOAT | METAL

6 February 1932 – 25 January 1933 | MONKEY | WATER

26 January 1933 – 13 February 1934 | ROOSTER | WATER
14 February 1934 – 3 February 1935 | DOG | WOOD
4 February 1935 – 23 January 1936 | PIG | WOOD
24 January 1936 – 10 February 1937 | RAT | FIRE
11 February 1937 – 30 January 1938 | OX | FIRE
31 January 1938 – 18 February 1939 | TIGER | EARTH
19 February 1939 – 7 February 1940 | RABBIT | EARTH

The 1940s

8 February 1940 – 26 January 1941 | DRAGON | METAL
27 January 1941 – 14 February 1942 | SNAKE | METAL
15 February 1942 – 4 February 1943 | HORSE | WATER
5 February 1943 – 24 January 1944 | GOAT | WATER
25 January 1944 – 12 February 1945 | MONKEY | WOOD
13 February 1945 – 1 February 1946 | ROOSTER | WOOD
2 February 1946 – 21 January 1947 | DOG | FIRE
22 January 1947 – 9 February 1948 | PIG | FIRE
10 February 1948 – 28 January 1949 | RAT | EARTH
29 January 1949 – 16 February 1950 | OX | EARTH

The 1950s

17 February 1950 – 5 February 1951 | TIGER | METAL
6 February 1951 – 26 January 1952 | RABBIT | METAL
27 January 1952 – 13 February 1953 | DRAGON | WATER
14 February 1953 – 2 February 1954 | SNAKE | WATER
3 February 1954 – 23 January 1955 | HORSE | WOOD
24 January 1955 – 11 February 1956 | GOAT | WOOD
12 February 1956 – 30 January 1957 | MONKEY | FIRE
31 January 1957 – 17 February 1958 | ROOSTER | FIRE
18 February 1958 – 7 February 1959 | DOG | EARTH
8 February 1959 – 27 January 1960 | PIG | EARTH

The 1960s

28 January 1960 – 14 February 1961 | RAT | METAL
15 February 1961 – 4 February 1962 | OX | METAL
5 February 1962 – 24 January 1963 | TIGER | WATER

25 January 1963 – 12 February 1964 | RABBIT | WATER
13 February 1964 – 1 February 1965 | DRAGON | WOOD
2 February 1965 – 20 January 1966 | SNAKE | WOOD
21 January 1966 – 8 February 1967 | HORSE | FIRE
9 February 1967 – 29 January 1968 | GOAT | FIRE
30 January 1968 – 16 February 1969 | MONKEY | EARTH
17 February 1969 – 5 February 1970 | ROOSTER | EARTH

The 1970s

6 February 1970 – 26 January 1971 | DOG | METAL
27 January 1971 – 14 February 1972 | PIG | METAL
15 February 1972 – 2 February 1973 | RAT | WATER
3 February 1973 – 22 January 1974 | OX | WATER
23 January 1974 – 10 February 1975 | TIGER | WOOD
11 February 1975 – 30 January 1976 | RABBIT | WOOD
31 January 1976 – 17 February 1977 | DRAGON | FIRE
18 February 1977 – 6 February 1978 | SNAKE | FIRE
7 February 1978 – 27 January 1979 | HORSE | EARTH
28 January 1979 – 15 February 1980 | GOAT | EARTH

The 1980s

16 February 1980 – 4 February 1981 | MONKEY | METAL
5 February 1981 – 24 January 1982 | ROOSTER | METAL
25 January 1982 – 12 February 1983 | DOG | WATER
13 February 1983 – 1 February 1984 | PIG | WATER
2 February 1984 – 19 February 1985 | RAT | WOOD
20 February 1985 – 8 February 1986 | OX | WOOD
9 February 1986 – 28 January 1987 | TIGER | FIRE
29 January 1987 – 16 February 1988 | RABBIT | FIRE
17 February 1988 – 5 February 1989 | DRAGON | EARTH
6 February 1989 – 26 January 1990 | SNAKE | EARTH

The 1990s

27 January 1990 – 14 February 1991 | HORSE | METAL
15 February 1991 – 3 February 1992 | GOAT | METAL
4 February 1992 – 22 January 1993 | MONKEY | WATER

23 January 1993 – 9 February 1994 | ROOSTER | WATER
10 February 1994 – 30 January 1995 | DOG | WOOD
31 January 1995 – 18 February 1996 | PIG | WOOD
19 February 1996 – 7 February 1997 | RAT | FIRE
8 February 1997 – 27 January 1998 | OX | FIRE
28 January 1998 – 5 February 1999 | TIGER | EARTH
6 February 1999 – 4 February 2000 | RABBIT | EARTH

The 2000s

5 February 2000 – 23 January 2001 | DRAGON | METAL
24 January 2001 – 11 February 2002 | SNAKE | METAL
12 February 2002 – 31 January 2003 | HORSE | WATER
1 February 2003 – 21 January 2004 | GOAT | WATER
22 January 2004 – 8 February 2005 | MONKEY | WOOD
9 February 2005 – 28 January 2006 | ROOSTER | WOOD
29 January 2006 – 17 February 2007 | DOG | FIRE
18 February 2007 – 6 February 2008 | PIG | FIRE
7 February 2008 – 25 January 2009 | RAT | EARTH
26 January 2009 – 13 February 2010 | OX | EARTH

The 2010s

14 February 2010 – 2 February 2011 | TIGER | METAL
3 February 2011 – 22 January 2012 | RABBIT | METAL
23 January 2012 – 9 February 2013 | DRAGON | WATER
10 February 2013 – 30 January 2014 | SNAKE | WATER
31 January 2014 – 18 February 2015 | HORSE | WOOD
19 February 2015 – 7 February 2016 | GOAT | WOOD
8 February 2016 – 27 January 2017 | MONKEY | FIRE
28 January 2017 – 15 February 2018 | ROOSTER | FIRE
16 February 2018 – 4 February 2019 | DOG | EARTH
5 February 2019 – 24 January 2020 | PIG | EARTH

The 2020s

25 January 2020 – 11 February 2021 | RAT | METAL
12 February 2021 – 1 February 2022 | OX | METAL
2 February 2022 – 21 January 2023 | TIGER | WATER

22 January 2023 – 9 February 2024 | RABBIT | WATER
10 February 2024 – 28 January 2025 | DRAGON | WOOD
29 January 2025 – 16 February 2026 | SNAKE | WOOD
17 February 2026 – 5 February 2027 | HORSE | FIRE
6 February 2027 – 25 January 2028 | GOAT | FIRE
26 January 2028 – 12 February 2029 | MONKEY | EARTH
13 February 2029 – 2 February 2030 | ROOSTER | EARTH

You may have noticed that the 'natural' basic element of your sign is not necessarily the same as the element of the year you were born. Don't worry about this. The element of your birth year takes precedence, though you could also read the qualities assigned to the natural element as well, as these will be relevant to your personality but to a lesser degree.

Metal

Metal is the element associated in China with gold and wealth. So, if you are a Metal child, you will be very good at accumulating money. The Metal individual is ambitious, even if their animal sign is not particularly career-minded. The Metal-born version of an unworldly sign will still somehow have an eye for a bargain or a good investment; they'll manage to buy at the right time when prices are low and be moved to sell just as the price is peaking. If they want to get rid of unwanted items, they'll potter along to a car boot sale and without appearing to try, somehow make a killing, selling the lot while stalls around them struggle for attention. Career-minded signs with the element Metal have to be careful they don't overdo things. They have a tendency to become workaholics. Wealth will certainly flow, but it could be at the expense of family harmony and social life.

The element of Metal adds power, drive, and tenacity to whatever sign it influences so if you were born in a Metal year, you'll never lack cash for long.

Water

Water is the element associated with communication, creativity, and the emotions. Water has a knack of flowing around obstacles, finding routes that are not obvious to the naked eye and seeping into the smallest cracks. So if you're a Water child, you'll be very good at getting what you want in an oblique, unchallenging way. You are one of nature's lateral thinkers. You are also wonderful with people. You're sympathetic, empathetic, and can always find the right words at the right time. You can also be highly persuasive, but in such a subtle way nobody notices your influence or input. They think the whole thing was their own idea.

People born in Water years are very creative and extremely intuitive. They don't know where their inspiration comes from, but somehow ideas just pour into their brains. Many artists were born in Water years.

Animal signs that are normally regarded as a little impatient and tactless have their rough edges smoothed when they appear in a Water year. People born in these years will be more diplomatic, artistic, and amiable than other versions of their fellow signs. And if you were born in a naturally sensitive, emotional sign, in a Water year, you'll be so intuitive you're probably psychic. Yet just as water can fall as gentle nurturing rain, or a raging destructive flood, so Water types need to take care not to let their emotions run away with them or to allow themselves to use their persuasive skills to be too manipulative.

Wood

Wood is the element associated with growth and expansion. In Chinese astrology, Wood doesn't primarily refer to the inert variety used to make floorboards and furniture, it represents living, flourishing trees and smaller plants, all pushing out of the earth and growing towards the sky.

Wood is represented by the colour green, not brown. If you're a Wood child, you're likely to be honest, generous, and friendly. You think BIG and like to be involved in numerous projects, often at the same time.

Wood people are practical yet imaginative and able to enlist the support of others simply by the sincerity and enthusiasm with which they tackle their plans. Yet even though they're always busy with a project, they somehow radiate calm, stability, and confidence. There's a sense of the timeless serenity of a big old tree about Wood people. Other signs instinctively trust them and look to them for guidance.

Animal signs that could be prone to nervousness or impulsive behaviour tend to be calmer and more productive in Wood year versions, while signs whose natural element is also Wood could well end up leaders of vast teams or business empires. Wood people tend to sail smoothly through life, but they must guard against becoming either stubborn or unyielding as they grow older or alternatively, saying 'yes' to every new plan and overextending themselves.

Fire

Fire is the element associated with dynamism, strength, and persistence. Fire demands action, movement, and expansion. It also creates a huge amount of heat. Fire is precious when it warms our homes and cooks our food, and it possesses a savage beauty that's endlessly fascinating. Yet it's also highly dangerous and destructive if it gets out of control. Something of this ambivalent quality is evident in Fire children.

People born in Fire years tend to be immensely attractive, magnetic types. Other signs are drawn to them. Yet there is always a hint of danger, of unpredictability, about them. You never know quite where you are with a Fire year sign and in a way, this is part of their fascination.

People born in Fire years like to get things done. They are extroverted and bold and impatient for action. They are brilliant at getting things started and energising people and projects. Quieter signs born in a Fire year are more dynamic, outspoken, and energetic than their fellow sign cousins, while extrovert signs positively blaze with exuberance and confidence when Fire is added to the mix.

People born in Fire years will always be noticed, but they should try to remember they tend to be impatient and impulsive. Develop a habit of pausing to take a deep breath to consider things, before rushing in, and you won't get burned.

Earth

Earth is the element associated with patience, stability, and practicality. This may not sound exciting but, in Chinese astrology, Earth is at the centre of everything: the heart of the planet. Earth year children are strong, hardworking personalities. They will persist with a task if it's worthwhile and never give up until it's complete. They create structure and balance, and they have very nurturing instincts.

Women born in Earth years make wonderful mothers, and if they're not mothering actual children, they'll be mothering their colleagues at work, or their friends and relatives, while also filling their homes with houseplants and raising vegetables in the garden if at all possible.

Other signs like being around Earth types as they exude a sense of security. Earth people don't like change, and they strive to keep their lives settled and harmonious. They are deeply kind and caring and immensely honest. Tact is not one of their strong points, however. They will always say what they think, so if you don't want the unvarnished truth, better not to ask!

Earth lends patience and stability to the more flighty, over-emotional signs, and rock-solid integrity to the others. Earth people will be sought-after in whatever field they choose to enter, but they must take care not to become too stubborn. Make a point of seeking out and listening to a wide range of varying opinions before setting a decision in stone.

Yin and Yang

As you looked down the table of years and elements, you may have noticed that the elements came in pairs. Each element was repeated the following year. If the Monkey was Water one year, it would be followed immediately the next year by the Rooster, also Water.

This is because of Yin and Yang – the mysterious but vital forces that, in Chinese philosophy, are believed to control the planet and probably the whole universe. They can be thought of as positive and negative, light and dark, masculine and feminine, night and day, etc. but the important point is that everything is either Yin or Yang; the two forces complement each other and both are equally important because only together do they make up the whole. For peace and harmony to be achieved, both forces need to be in balance.

Each of the animal signs is believed to be either Yin or Yang and because of the need for balance and harmony, they alternate through the years. Six of the 12 signs are Yin and six are Yang and since Yang represents extrovert, dominant energy, the Yang sign is first, followed by the Yin sign which represents quiet, passive force. A Yang sign is always followed by a Yin sign throughout the cycle.

The Yang signs are:

Rat

Tiger

Dragon

Horse

Monkey

Dog

The Yin Signs are

Ox

Rabbit

Snake

Goat

Rooster

Pig

Although Yang is seen as a masculine energy, and Yin a feminine energy, in reality, whether you are male or female, everyone has a mixture of Yin and Yang within them. If you need to know, quickly, whether your sign is Yin or Yang just check your birth year. If it ends in an even number (or 0) your sign is Yang. If it ends in an odd number, your sign is Yin. (The only exception is if you're born in late January or early February and according to Chinese astrology you belong to the year before).

In general, Yang signs tend to be extrovert, action-oriented types while Yin signs are gentler, more thoughtful, and patient.

So, as balance is essential when an element controls a period of time, it needs to express itself in its stronger Yang form in a Yang year as well as in its gentler Yin form in a Yin year, to be complete.

This year of the Green Wood Snake completes the round of the Wood element. Last year it was in its Yang form accompanied by the Dragon, now it draws to a close in its Yin form with the Wood Snake.

Next year the two year Fire element will begin. Followed by two Earth years, then two Metal years, two Water years and finally back to the Wood years again.

But why do elements have two forms? It's to take into account the great variations in strength encompassed by an element. The difference between a candle flame and a raging inferno – both belonging to Fire; or a great oak tree and a blade of grass – both belonging to the Wood element. Each has to get its turn to be expressed to create balance.

So, in Yang years, the influence of the ruling element will be particularly strong. In Yin years, the same element expresses itself in its gentler form.

Friendly Elements

Just as some signs get on well together and others don't, so some elements work well together while others don't. These are the elements that exist in harmony:

METAL likes EARTH and WATER

WATER likes METAL and WOOD

WOOD likes WATER and FIRE

FIRE likes WOOD and EARTH

EARTH likes FIRE and METAL

The reason for these friendly partnerships is believed to be the natural, productive cycle. Water nourishes Wood and makes plants grow, Wood provides fuel for Fire, Fire produces ash which is a type of Earth, Earth can be melted or mined to produce Metal while Metal contains or carries Water in a bucket.

So, Water supports Wood, Wood supports Fire, Fire supports Earth, Earth supports Metal and Metal supports Water.

Unfriendly Elements

But since everything has to be in balance, all the friendly elements are opposed by the same number of unfriendly elements. These are the elements that are not in harmony:

METAL dislikes WOOD and FIRE

WATER dislikes FIRE and EARTH

WOOD dislikes EARTH and METAL

FIRE dislikes METAL and WATER

EARTH dislikes WOOD and WATER

The reason some elements don't get on, is down to the destructive cycle which is: Water puts out Fire and is absorbed by Earth, Wood breaks up Earth (with its strong roots) and is harmed by Metal tools, Metal is melted by Fire and can cut down Wood.

So, if someone just seems to rub you up the wrong way, for no logical reason, it could be that your elements clash.

CHAPTER 16: WESTERN HOROSCOPES AND CHINESE HOROSCOPES – THE LINK

So now, hopefully, you'll have all the tools you need to create your very own, personal, multi-faceted Chinese horoscope. But does that mean the Western-style astrological sign that you're more familiar with is no longer relevant?

Not necessarily. Purists may not agree, but the odd thing is there does seem to be an overlap between a person's Western birth sign and their Chinese birth month sign; the two together can add yet another interesting layer to the basic birth year personality.

A Rabbit born under the Western sign of Leo may turn out to be very different on the surface, to a Rabbit born under the Western sign of Pisces for instance.

Of course, Chinese astrology already takes this into account by including the season of birth in a full chart, but we can possibly refine the system even further by adding the characteristics we've learned from our Western Sun Signs into the jigsaw.

If you'd like to put this theory to the test, simply find your Chinese year sign and then look up your Western Astrological sign within it, from the list below. While you're at it, why not check out the readings for your partner and friends too? You could be amazed at how accurate the results turn out to be.

Snake

Aries Snake

Generally speaking, Snakes tend to lack energy, so the influence of dynamic Aries is very welcome indeed. These subjects are highly intelligent, well-motivated and never leave anything unfinished. They are achievers and will not give up until they reach their goal – which they invariably do. Nothing can stand in the way of Aries Snakes, and they reach the top of whatever tree they climb.

Taurus Snake

In contrast, the sensuous Taurus Snake really can't be bothered with all that hard work. Taurus Snakes have great ability, but they will only do as much as is necessary to acquire the lifestyle they desire, and then they like to sit back and enjoy it. Tremendous sun worshippers, the Taurus Snakes would be quite happy to be on a permanent holiday, providing the accommodation was a five-star hotel with a fabulous restaurant.

Gemini Snake

The Gemini Snake can be a slippery customer. A brilliant brain, linked to a shrewd but amusing tongue, these types can run rings around almost everybody. They can scheme and manipulate if it suits them and pull off all sorts of audacious tricks but having achieved much, they tend to get bored and lose interest, giving up on the brink of great things. This often leads to conflict with business associates who cannot understand such contradictory behaviour. Insane they call it. Suicidal. The Gemini Snake just shrugs and moves on.

Cancer Snake

The Snake born under the sign of Cancer is a more conventional creature. These types will at least do all that is required of them and bring their formidable Snake brains to bear on the task in hand. They are gifted researchers, historians and archaeologists – any career which involves deep concentration and patient study. But the Cancer Snake must take care to mix with cheerful people since left to himself he has a tendency for melancholy. Warmth, laughter, and plenty of rest transforms the Cancer Snake and allows those unique talents to blossom.

Leo Snake

The Leo Snake is a very seductive creature. Beautifully dressed, sparklingly magnetic, few people can take their eyes off these types, and they know it. All Snakes are sensuous, but the Snake born under the sign of Leo is probably the most sensuous of the lot. Never short of admirers, these types are not eager to settle down. Why should they when they're having such a good time? Late in life, the Leo Snake may consent to get married if their partner can offer them a good enough life. If not, these types are quite content to go it alone – probably because they are never truly on their own. They collect willing followers right into old age.

Virgo Snake

The Virgo Snake is another fascinating combination. Highly intuitive and wildly passionate, the Virgo Snake is all elegant understatement on the outside and erotic abandon on the inside. The opposite sex is mesmerised by this intriguing contradiction and just can't stay away. Virgo Snakes can achieve success in their careers if they put their minds to it, but often they are having too much fun flirting and flitting from one lover to the next. Faithfulness is not their strong point, but they are so sexy they get away with murder.

Libra Snake

When you see a top model slinking sinuously down the catwalk, she could very well be a Libra Snake. Snakes born under this sign are the most elegant and stylish of the lot. They may not be conventionally good looking, but they will turn heads wherever they go. These types really understand clothes and could make a plastic bin-liner look glamorous just by putting it on. Somehow, they have the knack of stepping off a transatlantic flight without a crease and driving an open-topped sports car without ruffling their hair. No-one knows quite how they achieve these feats, and Libra Snake isn't telling.

Scorpio Snake

The Snake born under Scorpio is destined to have a complicated life. These types enjoy plots and intrigues, particularly of a romantic nature and spend endless hours devising schemes and planning subterfuge. That ingenious Snake brain is capable of brewing up the most elaborate scams, and there's nothing Scorpio Snake loves more than watching all the parts fall into place. But schemes have a knack of going wrong, and schemers have to change their plans and change them again to cope with each new contingency as it arises. If he's not careful, the Scorpio Snake can become hopelessly embroiled in his own plot.

Sagittarius Snake

Traditionally other signs are wary of the Snake and tend to hold back a little from them without knowing why. When the Snake is born under Sagittarius, however, the subject seems more approachable than most. Sagittarian Snakes sooner or later become recognised for their wisdom and down to earth good sense and people flock to them for advice. Without ever intending to, the Sagittarius Snake could end up as something of a guru attracting eager acolytes desperate to learn more.

Capricorn Snake

The Snake born under Capricorn is more ambitious than the average serpent. These types will reach for the stars and grasp them. Obstacles just melt away when faced with the dual-beam of Capricorn Snake intelligence and quiet persistence. These Snakes are good providers and more dependable than most Snakes. They often end up surrounded by all the trappings of success, but they accomplish this so quietly, no one can quite work out how they managed it.

Aquarius Snake

Another highly intuitive Snake. Independent but people-loving Aquarius endows the serpent with greater social skills than usual. These types attract many friends, and they have the ability to understand just how others are feeling without them having to say a word. These Snakes have particularly enquiring minds, and they can't pass a museum or book shop without going in to browse. Born researchers, they love to dig and delve into whatever subject has taken their fancy, no matter how obscure. Quite often, they discover something valuable by accident.

Pisces Snake

Pisces Snakes tend to live on their nerves even more than most. These types are friendly up to a point, but they hate disagreements and problems and withdraw when things look unpleasant. They are sexy and sensuous and would much prefer a quiet evening with just one special person than a wild party. In the privacy of their bedroom, anything goes, and Pisces Snakes reveal the naughty side of their characters. No one would guess from the understated elegance of their exteriors what an erotic creature the Pisces Snake really is.

Horse

Aries Horse

Overflowing with energy the Aries Horse just can't sit still for long. These types just have to find an outlet for their phenomenal vitality. They are hardworking, hard-playing, and usually highly popular. Less fun-loving signs might be accused of being workaholics but not the Aries Horse. People born under this sign devote enormous amounts of time to their careers but still have so much spare capacity there is plenty left over for their friends. They always do well in their chosen profession.

Taurus Horse

The Taurus Horse can be a trickier creature. Charming yet logical, he has a very good brain and is not afraid to use it. The only problem is that without warning the Taurus Horse can turn from flighty and fun to immensely stubborn and even an earthquake wouldn't shift him from an entrenched position. Yet treated with understanding and patience, the Taurus Horse can be coaxed to produce wonderful achievements.

Gemini Horse

Gemini types are easily bored, and when they are born in the freedom-loving year of the Horse, this trait tends to be accentuated. Unless their attention is caught and held almost instantly, Gemini Horse subjects kick up their heels and gallop off to find more fun elsewhere. For this reason, they often find it difficult to hold on to a job, and they change careers frequently. Yet once they discover a subject about which they can feel passionate, they employ the whole of their considerable talent and will zoom to the top in record time.

Cancer Horse

The Cancer Horse is a lovable creature with a great many friends. These types tend to lack confidence and need a lot of praise and nurturing, but with the right leadership, they will move mountains. Some signs find them difficult to understand because the Cancer Horse loves to be surrounded by a crowd yet needs a lot of alone time too. Misjudge the mood, and the Cancer Horse can seem bafflingly unfriendly. Yet, stay the course, and these subjects become wonderfully loyal friends.

Leo Horse

People born under the star sign of Leo will be the first to admit they like to show off and when they are also born in the year of the Horse, they enjoy showing off all the more. These types love nothing better than strutting around rocking designer outfits while others look on in admiration. They are not so interested in home decor; it's their own personal appearance which counts most. The Leo Horse would much rather invest time and money boosting their image than shoving their earnings into a bank account to gather dust.

Virgo Horse

Virgo types can be a little solemn and over-devoted to duty, but when they are born in the year of the Horse, they are endowed with a welcome streak of equine frivolity. The Virgo Horse loves to party. He will make sure his work is completed first of course, but once the office door clicks shut behind him, the Virgo Horse really knows how to let his hair down.

Libra Horse

The Libra Horse is another true charmer. Friends and acquaintances by the score fill the address books of these types, and their diaries are crammed with appointments. Honest, trustworthy and helpful, other people can't help gravitating to them. Oddly enough, despite their gregarious nature, these types are also very independent. Sometimes too independent for their own good. They are excellent at giving advice to others but find it almost impossible to take advice themselves.

Scorpio Horse

The Scorpio Horse is a real thrill seeker. These types enjoy life's pleasures, particularly passionate pleasures and go all out to attain them. There is no middle road with the Scorpio Horse. These are all or nothing types. They fling themselves into the project of the moment wholeheartedly or not at all. They tend to see things in black and white and believe others are either for them or against them. In serious moments, the Scorpio Horse subscribes to some surprising conspiracy theories, but mostly they keep these ideas to themselves.

Sagittarius Horse

The star sign of Sagittarius is the sign of the Centaur – half-man half-horse – and when these types are born in the year of the Horse, the equine tendencies are so strong they practically have four hooves. Carefree country-lovers these subjects can't bear to be penned in and never feel totally happy until they are out of doors in some wide-open space. They crave fresh air and regular exercise and do best in joint activities. As long as they can spend enough time out of doors, Sagittarius Horses are blessed with glowing good health.

Capricorn Horse

The Capricorn Horse is a canny beast. These types are great savers. They manage to have fun on a shoestring and stash away every spare penny at the same time. They are prepared to work immensely hard provided the pay is good, and they have a remarkable knack of finding just the right job to make the most of their earning power. The Capricorn Horse likes a good time, and he will never be poor.

Aquarius Horse

When Aquarius meets the Horse, it results in a very curious creature. These types admit to enquiring minds; other less charitable signs might call them nosey parkers. Call them what you may, subjects born under this sign need to know and discover. They often become inventors, and they have a weakness for new gadgets and the latest technology. The Aquarius Horse can be wildly impractical and annoy partners by frittering cash away on their latest obsession. They also tend to fill their living space with peculiar objects from junk shops and car boot sales, which they intend to upcycle into useful treasures. Somehow, they seldom get round to finishing the project.

Pisces Horse

Artistic Pisces adds an unusual dimension to the physical Horse, who normally has little time for cultural frills and foibles. These types are great home entertainers and often gifted cooks as well. They invite a group of friends around at the slightest excuse and can conjure delicious snacks and drinks from the most unpromising larders. They adore company and get melancholy if left alone too long.

Goat

Aries Goat

Normally mild and unassuming, the Goat can become almost argumentative when born under the star sign of Aries. Though friendly and very seldom cross, the Aries Goat will suddenly adopt an unexpectedly stubborn position and stick to it unreasonably even when it's obvious he is wrong. Despite this, these types are blessed with sunny natures and are quickly forgiven. They don't bear a grudge and have no idea – after the awkwardness – that anything unpleasant occurred.

Taurus Goat

Like his Aries cousin, the Taurus Goat can turn stubborn too. These types have a very long fuse. Most people would assume they did not have a temper because it is so rarely displayed. But make them truly angry, and they will explode. Small they may be, but a raging Goat can be a fearful sight. On the other hand, these Goats are more likely to have a sweet tooth than their cousins, so if you do upset them, a choccy treat could work wonders in making amends.

Gemini Goat

The Goat born under Gemini is a terrible worrier. These types seem to use their active minds to dream up all the troubles and problems that could result from every single action. Naturally, this renders decision-making almost impossible. They dither and rethink and ponder until finally someone else makes up their mind for them, at which point they are quite happy. In fact, if the Gemini Goat never had to make another decision, she would be a blissfully content creature.

Cancer Goat

Gentle, soft-hearted and kind, the Cancer Goat is a friend to all in need. These types would give their last penny to a homeless beggar in the street, and they always have a shoulder ready should anyone need to cry on it. Yet they can also be surprisingly moody for what appears to be no reason at all, and this characteristic can be baffling to their friends. No point in wasting time asking what's wrong, they find it difficult to explain. Just wait for the clouds to pass.

Leo Goat

The Leo Goat is a very fine specimen. Warm, friendly and more extrovert than her quieter Goat cousins, she seems to have the confidence other Goats often lack. Look more closely though, and you can find all is not quite as it seems. Frequently, that self-assured appearance is merely a well-presented 'front'. Back in the privacy of their own home, the bold Leo Goat can crumble. In truth, these types are easily hurt.

Virgo Goat

Outwardly vague and preoccupied, the Virgo Goat can turn unexpectedly fussy. These types are easy-going, but they can't stand messy homes, mud in their car or sweet wrappers lying around. Yet they would be genuinely surprised if anyone accused them of being pernickety. They believe they are laid back and good-humoured, which they are. Just don't drop chewing gum on their front path, that's all, and take your shoes off at the door.

Libra Goat

The Libra Goat is obliging to the point of self-sacrifice. These types are truly nice people. Generous with their time as well as their possessions. Unfortunately, their good nature is sometimes exploited by the unscrupulous. The Libra Goat will wear itself out in the service of those in distress, will refuse to hear a bad word about anyone and will remain loyal to friends despite the most intense provocation. The Libra Goat lives to please.

Scorpio Goat

Scorpio Goats are among the most strong-willed of all the Goats. They like to go their own way and hate to have others tell them what to do. They don't mind leaving irksome chores and duties to others, but woe betides anyone who tries to interfere with the Scorpio Goat's pet project. At first sight, they may appear preoccupied and have their heads in the clouds, but beneath that vague exterior, their sharp eyes miss very little. Don't underestimate the Scorpio Goat.

Sagittarius Goat

Sagittarius lends an adventurous streak to the normally cautious Goat make-up, and these types tend to take far more risks than their cousins born at other times of the year. While they still enjoy being taken care of, the Sagittarius Goat prefers cosseting on his return from adventures, not instead of them. These types are often good in business and amaze everyone by doing 'extremely well' apparently by accident.

Capricorn Goat

The Capricorn Goat, in contrast, is a very cautious creature. Danger beckons at every turn and security is top of their list of priorities. This Goat can never get to sleep until every door and window has been locked and secured. Should they find themselves staying in a hotel, Capricorn Goats will often drag a chair in front of the bedroom door, just in case. These types are difficult to get to know because it takes a while to win their trust, but once they become friends, they will be loyal forever and despite their caution – or sensible outlook as they'd call it – they can be very successful.

Aquarius Goat

The Aquarius Goat tends to leap about from one high-minded project to the next. These well-meaning types might be manning a soup kitchen one day and devising a scheme to combat climate change the next. Their grand plans seldom come to fruition because they find the practical details so difficult to put into operation but should they link up with an organisational genius they could achieve great things.

Pisces Goat

The Pisces Goat is a very sensitive soul. These types are often highly gifted, and their best course of action is to find someone to take care of them as soon as possible so that they can get on with cultivating their talents. Left to themselves Pisces Goats will neglect their physical needs, failing to cook proper meals or dress warmly in cold weather. With the right guidance, however, they can work wonders.

Monkey

Aries Monkey

These cheeky types have a charm that is quite irresistible. Energetic and mischievous they adore parties and social gatherings of any kind. They crop up on every guest list because they are so entertaining. The Aries Monkey is a font of funny stories and silly jokes but seldom stands still for long. Friends of the Aries Monkey are often frustrated as their popular companion is so in demand it's difficult to pin her down for a catch-up.

Taurus Monkey

The Monkey born under the star sign of Taurus has a little more weight in his character. These types take life a shade more seriously than their delightfully frivolous cousins. Not that the Taurus Monkey is ever a stick-in-the-mud. It's just that business comes before pleasure with these types, although only just, and the business that catches their eye is not necessarily what others would call business. Taurus Monkey is as captivated by creating a useful container out of an old coffee jar as checking out a balance sheet.

Gemini Monkey

The Gemini Monkey Is a true comedian. Incredibly quick-witted, these types only have to open their mouths, and everyone around them is in stitches. If Oscar Wilde was not a Gemini Monkey, he should have been. People born under this sign could easily make a career in the comedy field if they can be bothered to make enough attempts. Truth is they're just as happy entertaining their friends as a theatre full of people.

Cancer Monkey

These types have a gentler side to their characters. Cancer Monkey's love to tinker with machinery and see how things work. They tend to take things to pieces and then forget to put them together again. They are easily hurt, however, if someone complains about this trait. They genuinely intend to put things right. It is just that, somehow, they never manage to get round to it, and they never realise that this is a trait they repeat over and over again

Leo Monkey

The Leo Monkey is a highly adaptable creature. He can be all things to all men while still retaining his own unique personality. Popular, amusing and fond of practical jokes these types are welcome wherever they go. They can sometimes get rather carried away with the sound of their own voices and end up being rather tactless, but such is their charm that everyone forgives them. Occasionally, a practical joke can go too far, but kind-hearted Leo Monkey is horrified if anyone feels hurt, and instantly apologises.

Virgo Monkey

The Virgo Monkey could be a great inventor. The Monkey's natural ingenuity blends with Virgo's patience and fussiness over detail to create a character with the ideas to discover something new and the tenacity to carry on until it is perfected. If they could curb their impulse to rush on to the next brilliant idea when the last is complete, and turned their intention instead to marketing, they could make a fortune.

Libra Monkey

The Monkey born under the sign of Libra is actually a force to be reckoned with though no-one would ever guess it. These types are lovable and fun and have a knack of getting other people to do what they want without even realising they've been talked into it. In fact, Libran Monkeys are first-class manipulators but so skilled at their craft that nobody minds. These types could get away with murder.

Scorpio Monkey

Normally, the Monkey is a real chatterbox, but when Scorpio is added to the mix, you have a primate with the unusual gift of discretion right alongside his natural loquaciousness. These types will happily gossip all day long, but if they need to keep a secret, they are able to do so, to the grave if necessary. Scorpio Monkey could be an actor or a spy – and play each role to perfection. 007 could well have been a Scorpio Monkey.

Sagittarius Monkey

These flexible, amorous, adventure-loving Monkeys add zing to any gathering. These are the guests with the mad-cap ideas who want to jump fully clothed into the swimming pool at midnight and think it terrific fun to see in the New Year on top of Ben Nevis. It's difficult to keep up with the Sagittarius Monkey, but it's certainly fun to try.

Capricorn Monkey

Capricorn Monkeys have their serious side, but they are also flirty types. These are the subjects who charm with ease and tease and joke their conquests into bed. The trouble is Capricorn Monkey often promises more than is deliverable. These types tire more easily than they realise, and can't always put their exciting schemes into action. This rarely stops them trying, of course.

Aquarius Monkey

The Aquarius Monkey is a particularly inventive creature and employs his considerable intellect in trying to discover new ways to save the world. These types often have a hard time in their early years as it takes them decades to realise that not everyone sees the importance of their passions as they do. But, once they understand a different approach is needed, they go on to accomplish much in later life.

Pisces Monkey

The Pisces Monkey can be a puzzling creature. These types are dreamy and amusing one minute and irritable and quick-tempered the next. They can go with the flow so far and then suddenly wonder why no-one can keep up with them when they decide to get a move on. They tend to lack quite so much humour when the joke is on themselves, but most of the time they are agreeable companions.

Rooster

Aries Rooster

Stand well back when confronted with an Aries Rooster. These types are one hundred percent go-getter, and nothing will stand in their way. Aries Rooster can excel at anything to which he puts his mind, and as he frequently puts his mind to business matters, he's likely to end up a billionaire. Think scarlet sports cars, ostentatious homes, and a personal helicopter or two – the owner is bound to be an Aries Rooster.

Taurus Rooster

The Taurus Rooster has a heart of gold but can come over as a bit of a bossy boots, particularly in financial matters. These types believe they have a unique understanding of money and accounts and are forever trying to get more sloppy signs to sharpen up in this department. Even if their manner rankles, it's worth listening to their advice. Annoyingly, they are often right.

Gemini Rooster

The Rooster born under the sign of Gemini would make a terrific private detective were it not for the fact that Roosters find it almost impossible to blend into the background. Gemini Roosters love to find out what's going on and have an uncanny ability to stumble on the one thing you don't wish them to know. They mean no harm, however, and once they find a suitable outlet for their talents, they will go far.

Cancer Rooster

The Rooster born under the sign of Cancer is often a fine-looking creature and knows it. These types are secretly rather vain and behind the scenes take great pains with their appearance. They would die rather than admit it, however, and like to give the impression that their wonderful style is no more than a happy accident. Though they cultivate a relaxed, easy-going manner, a bad hair day or a splash of mud on their new suede boots is enough to send them into a major sulk for hours.

Leo Rooster

Not everyone takes to the Leo Rooster. The Lion is a naturally proud, extrovert sign and when allied to the strutting Rooster, there is a danger of these types ending up as bossy exhibitionists. Yet they really have the kindest of hearts and will leap from their pedestals in an instant to comfort someone who seems upset. A word of warning – they should avoid excessive alcohol as these types can get merry on a sniff of a cider apple.

Virgo Rooster

The Virgo Rooster is a hardworking, dedicated creature, devoted to family, but in an undemonstrative way. Wind this bird up at your peril, however. These types have little sense of humour when it comes to taking a joke, and they will hold a grudge for months if they feel someone has made them look foolish. They hate to be laughed at.

Libra Rooster

The Libra Rooster likes to look good, have a fine home and share his considerable assets with his closest friends. These types enjoy admiration, but they are more subtle than Leo Roosters and don't demand it quite so openly. Libra Rooster is quite happy to give but does expect gratitude in return.

Scorpio Rooster

The Scorpio Rooster is a heroic creature. These types will defend a position to the death. In days of old, many a Scorpio Rooster will have got involved in a duel because these types cannot endure insults, will fight aggression with aggression and will not back down under any circumstances. Foolhardy they may appear, but there is something admirable about them nevertheless.

Sagittarius Rooster

The Sagittarius Rooster tends to be a little excitable and rash. These types are bold and brash and ready for anything. They love to travel and are desperate to see what's over the next hill and around the next bend. Born explorers' they never want to tread the conventional travel path. Let others holiday in Marbella if they wish. Sagittarius Rooster prefers a walking tour of Tibet.

Capricorn Rooster

Capricorn brings a steadying quality to the impulsive Rooster. These types like to achieve, consolidate, and then build again. They believe they are amassing a fortune for their family and they usually do. However, sometimes, their families would prefer a little less security and more attention. Best not to mention it to Capricorn Rooster though – this Rooster is likely to feel hurt and offended.

Aquarius Rooster

The Aquarius Rooster is frequently misunderstood. These types mean well but they tend to be impulsive and speak before they think, accidentally offending others when they do so. In fact, the Aquarius Rooster is a sensitive creature beneath that brash exterior and is easily hurt. If they can learn to count to ten before saying anything controversial, and maybe rephrase, they'd be amazed at how successful they'd become.

Pisces Rooster

The Pisces Rooster has a secret fear. He is terrified that one day he will be terribly poor. These types save hard to stave off that dreadful fate and will only feel totally relaxed when they have a huge nest egg behind them. Despite this, they manage to fall in and out of love regularly and often end up delighting their partners with the wonderful lifestyle they can create.

Dog

Aries Dog

The Aries Dog is a friendly type. Extrovert and sociable these subjects like a lively career and cheerful home life. They are not excessively materialistic, but they tend to make headway in the world without trying too hard. Aries Dog likes to get things done and will bound from one task to the next with energy and enthusiasm.

Taurus Dog

The Dog born under the star sign of Taurus is the most dependable creature in the world. Their word really is their bond, and they will never break a promise while there is breath in their body. They tend to be ultra-conservative with a small 'c'. The men are inclined to be chauvinists, and the women usually hold traditional views. They really do prefer to make their home and family their priority. They are loyal and kind, and people instinctively trust them.

Gemini Dog

The Gemini Dog, in contrast, while never actually dishonest, can be a bit of a sly fox when necessary. The quickest of all Dogs, the Gemini breed gets impatient when the going gets slow and resorts to the odd trick to speed things along. Nevertheless, these types are truthful and honest in their own way and have a knack of falling on their feet... whatever happens.

Cancer Dog

The Cancer Dog was born to be in a settled relationship. These types are never totally happy until they've found their true love and built a cosy home to snuggle up in together. Cancer Dog is not overly concerned with a career. As long as these types earn enough to pay the mortgage and buy life's essentials, they are happy. The right companionship is what they crave. With the perfect partner by their side, they are truly content.

Leo Dog

If Leo Dogs really did have four legs, chances are they would be police dogs. These types are sticklers for law and order. They will not tolerate injustice and will seek out wrongdoers and plague them until they change their ways. Woe betide any workmate who is pilfering pens, making free with office coffee or fiddling expenses. The Leo Dog will force them to own up and make amends. Should you be a victim of injustice, however, Leo Dog will zoom to your aid.

Virgo Dog

The Virgo Dog tends to be a great worrier. A born perfectionist, Virgo Dog agonises over every detail and loses sleep if he suspects he has performed any task badly. These types are very clever and can achieve great things, but too often they fail to enjoy their success because they are too busy worrying they might have made a mistake. The crazy thing is, they very seldom do.

Libra Dog

The Libra Dog believes in 'live and let live'. A laid back, tolerant fellow, Libra Dog likes to lie in the sun and not interfere with anyone. Let sleeping dogs lie is definitely her motto. She will agree to almost anything for a quiet life. Yet it's unwise to push her too far. When there's no alternative, this particular hound can produce a very loud bark.

Scorpio Dog

The Scorpio Dog is as loyal and trustworthy as other canines, but more difficult to get to know. Beneath that amiable exterior is a very suspicious heart. These types don't quite understand why they are so wary of others, but it takes them a long time to learn to trust. Perhaps they are afraid of getting hurt. The idea of marriage fills them with terror, and it takes a very patient partner to get them to the altar. Once married, however, they will be faithful and true.

Sagittarius Dog

The Sagittarius Dog is inexhaustible. These cheerful types are always raring to go and quite happy to join in with any adventure. They love to be part of the gang and are perfectly willing to follow someone else's lead. They don't mind if their ideas are not always accepted; they just like being involved. These types work splendidly in teams and can achieve great things in a group.

Capricorn Dog

The Capricorn Dog is a very caring type. These subjects are happy so long as their loved ones are happy, but they greatly fear that a friend or family member might fall ill. This concern, probably kept secret, gives them real anxiety and should a loved one show worrying symptoms, the Capricorn Dog will suffer sleepless nights until the problem is resolved. When they are not urging their families to keep warm and put on an extra vest, these types are likely to be out and about helping others less fortunate than themselves.

Aquarius Dog

The Aquarius Dog, when young, spends a great deal of time searching for a worthy cause to which they can become devoted. Since there are so many worthy causes from which to choose these types can suffer much heartache as they struggle to pick the right one. When – at last – a niche is found, however, the Aquarius Dog will settle down to a truly contented life of quiet satisfaction. These types need to serve and feel that they are improving life for others. This is their path to happiness.

Pisces Dog

Like the Aquarius breed, the Pisces Dog often has a number of false starts early in life although these are more likely to be of a romantic rather than philanthropic nature. The Pisces Dog wants to find a soulmate but is not averse to exploring a few cul-de-sacs on the way. These types are not promiscuous, however, and when they do find Mr or Miss Right, they are blissfully happy to settle down.

Pig

Aries Pig

The Aries Pig always seems to wear a smile on its face and no wonder. Everything seems to go right for these cheerful types, and they scarcely seem to have to lift a finger to make things fall perfectly into place. In fact, of course, their good luck is the result of sheer hard work, but the Aries Pig has a knack of making work look like play so that nobody realises the effort Pig is putting in.

Taurus Pig

Most Pigs are happy, but the Taurus Pigs really seem quite blissful most of the time. One of their favourite occupations is eating, and they delight in dreaming up sumptuous menus and then creating them for the enjoyment of themselves and their friends. For this reason, Taurus Pigs have a tendency to put on weight. Despite the time they devote to their hobby, however, Taurus Pigs usually do well in their career. Many gifted designers are born under this sign.

Gemini Pig

The Gemini Pig has a brilliant business brain gift-wrapped in a charming, happy go lucky personality. These types usually zoom straight to the top of their chosen tree, but they manage to do so smoothly and easily without ruffling too many feathers on the way. They are popular with their workmates, and later their employees, and nobody can figure out how quite such a nice, down to earth type has ended up in such a position of authority.

Cancer Pig

The Cancer Pig likes to give the impression of being a very hard-working type. She is hard working, of course, but perhaps not quite as excessively as she likes others to believe. Secretly, the Cancer Pig makes sure there's plenty of time to spare for fun and indulgence. To the outside world, however, Pig pretends to be constantly slaving away and likes to get regular appreciation for these efforts.

Leo Pig

The Leo Pig is delightful company. Friendly, amusing and very warm and approachable. These types do however have a tremendously lazy streak. Left to themselves, they would not rise till noon, and they prefer someone else to do all the cleaning and cooking. The Leo Pig has to be nagged to make an effort, but when these types do so, they can achieve impressive results.

Virgo Pig

The Virgo Pig, in contrast, is a highly conscientious creature. These types can't abide laziness, and while they are normally kindly, helpful souls who gladly assist others, they will not lift a finger to aid someone who has brought his problems on himself through slovenliness. The Virgo Pig is a clean, contented type who usually achieves a happy life.

Libra Pig

The creative Libra Pig is always dreaming up new ways to improve their home. These types love to be surrounded by beautiful and comfortable things but seldom get round to completing their ideas because they are having such a good time in other ways. This is probably just as well because the minute they decide on one colour scheme, they suddenly see something that might work better. A permanent work in progress is probably the best option.

Scorpio Pig

The Scorpio Pig usually goes far. The amiable Pig boosted by powerful, almost psychic Scorpio can seem turbo-charged at times. These types keep their own counsel more than their chatty cousins, and this often stands them in good stead in business. They can be a little too cautious at times, but they rarely make mistakes.

Sagittarius Pig

Eat, drink and be merry is the motto of the Sagittarius Pig. These types have the intelligence to go far in their careers but, in truth, they would rather party. They love to dress up, get together with a bunch of friends and laugh and dance until dawn. Sagittarius Pig hates to be alone for long, so is always off in search of company.

Capricorn Pig

Pigs are normally broad-minded types, but the Capricorn Pig is a little more staid than his cousins. Nevertheless, being able to narrow their vision gives these types the ability to channel their concentration totally onto the subject in hand, a gift which is vital to success in many professions. For this reason, Capricorn Pigs often make a name for themselves in their chosen career.

Aquarius Pig

Honest, straightforward and popular Aquarius Pigs have more friends than they can count. Always good-humoured and cheerful these types gravitate to those in need and do whatever they can to help. The Aquarius Pig gives copiously to charity and frequently wishes to do more. These types tend to have their heads in the clouds most of the time and for this reason, tend not to give their careers or finances the attention they should. But since worldly success means little to the Aquarius Pig, this hardly matters.

Pisces Pig

The Pisces Pig is a particularly sweet-natured creature. These types are real dreamers. They float around in a world of their own, and people tend to make allowances for them. Yet, from time to time, the Pisces Pig drifts in from his other planet to startle everyone with a stunningly brilliant idea. There is more to the Pisces Pig than meets the eye.

Rat

Aries Rat

Fiery Aries adds more than usual urgency to the sociable Rat. While these types enjoy company, they also tend to be impatient and can get quite bad-tempered and aggressive with anyone who seems to waste their time. Aries Rats do not suffer fools and will stomp off on their own if someone annoys them. In fact, this is the best thing all round. Aries Rats hate to admit it, but they benefit from a little solitude which enables them to calm down and recharge their batteries. Happily, as quickly as these types flare up, they just as quickly cool off again.

Taurus Rat

When Taurus, renowned for a love of luxury and the finer things in life, is born in a comfort-loving Rat year, a true gourmet and bon viveur has entered the world. The Taurus effect enhances the sensuous parts of the Rat personality and lifts them to new heights. Good food is absolutely essential to these types. They don't eat to live; they really do live to eat. Many excellent chefs are born under this sign, and even those folks who don't make catering their career are likely to be outstanding home cooks. Dinner parties thrown by Taurus Rats are memorable affairs. The only drawback with these types is that they can become a little pernickety and overly fussy about details. They also have to watch their weight.

Gemini Rat

While Taurus accentuates the Rat's love of good living, Gemini heightens the Rat's already well-developed social skills. That crowd chuckling and laughing around the witty type in the corner are bound to be listening to a Gemini Rat. Amusing, quick-thinking, and never lost for words, the only things likely to drive Gemini Rats away are bores and undue seriousness. Gemini Rats prefer light, entertaining conversation and head for the hills when things get too heavy. Delightful as they always are however, it is difficult to capture the attention of a Gemini Rat for long. These types love to circulate. They make an entrance and then move on to pastures new. Pinning them down never works. They simply lose interest and with it that famous sparkle.

Cancer Rat

Cancer makes the Rat a little more sensitive and easily hurt than usual. These types are emotional and loving but sometimes come across as martyrs. They work hard but tend to feel, often without good cause, their efforts are not as well appreciated as they should be. Cancer Rats frequently suspect they are being taken for granted at home and at work, but their love of company prevents them from making too big a fuss. Rats are naturally gifted business people, and the Cancer Rat has a particularly good head for financial affairs. These types enjoy working with others, and they are especially well suited to partnerships. However, don't expect the sensitive, feeling Cancer Rat to be a pushover. These types can be surprisingly demanding at work and will not tolerate any laziness on the part of employees.

Leo Rat

Leo Rats usually get to the top. Few people can resist them. The combination of Rat sociability, business acumen and ambition, coupled with extrovert Leo's rather, shall we say, 'pushy', qualities and flair for leadership can't help but power these types to the top of whatever tree they happen to choose to climb. Along the way, however, they may irritate those few less gifted souls who fail to fall under their spell. Such doubters may complain that Leo Rat hogs the limelight and tends to become overbearing at times but since hardly anyone else seems to notice, why should Leo Rat care?

Virgo Rat

As we have already seen, the delightful Rat does have a stingy streak in his make-up, and when the astrological sign of Virgo is added to the mix, this characteristic tends to widen. At best, Virgo Rats are terrific savers and do wonders with their investments. The Rat tendency to squander money on unwise bargains is almost entirely absent in these types, and they often end up seriously rich. At worst, however, in negative types, Virgo Rats can be real Scrooges, grating the last sliver of soap to save on washing powder, sitting in the dark to conserve electricity and attempting their own shoe repairs with stick-on soles, even when they have plenty of money in the bank. Virgo Rats are brilliant at detail; but in negative types, they put this gift to poor use spending far too long on money-saving schemes when they would do much better to look for ways of expanding their income.

Libra Rat

The Libra Rat adores company even more than most. In fact, these types are seldom alone. They have dozens of friends, their phones never stop ringing, and most evenings the Libra Rat is entertaining. Libra Rat enjoys civilised gatherings rather than wild parties and friends will be treated to beautiful music, exquisite food and a supremely comfortable home. These types really can charm the birds off the trees, not with the brilliant repartee of the Gemini Rat but with a warmth and low-key humour all their own. These types do tend to be a touch lazier than the usual Rat and their weakness for bargains, particularly in the areas of art and fashion, is more pronounced, but their charm is so strong that partners forgive them for overspending.

Scorpio Rat

It's often said that Rats would make good journalists or detectives because beneath that expansive surface is a highly observant brain. Well the best of them all would be the Rat born under Scorpio. A veritable

Sherlock Holmes of a Rat if you wish to be flattering, or a real nosey parker if you don't. These types are endlessly curious. They want to know everything that's going on, who is doing what with whom where and for how long. They may not have any particular use for the information they gather, but they just can't help gathering it all the same. Scorpio Rats often have psychic powers though they may not be aware of this and these powers aid them in their 'research'. Unlike other Rats, those born under Scorpio prefer their own company and like to work alone. When they manage to combine their curiosity and talent for digging out information, there is almost no limit to what they can achieve with their career

Sagittarius Rat

Traditionally Rats have many friends, but the Sagittarius Rat has the not so welcome distinction of collecting a few enemies along the way as well. The Sagittarius Rat finds this quite extraordinary as he never intends to upset anyone. It's just that these types can be forthright to the point of rudeness and an affable nature can only compensate so far. These types are amicable and warm, but when they speak their minds, some people never forgive them. Despite this tendency, Sagittarius Rats have a knack for accumulating money and plough it back into their business to good effect. They manage to be generous, and a bit mean at the same time, which baffles their friends, but those that have not been offended by Sagittarius Rat's tactless tongue tend to stay loyal forever.

Capricorn Rat

Rats are naturally high achievers, but perhaps the highest achiever of them all is likely to be born under the sign of Capricorn. These types are not loud and brilliant like Leo Rats. They tend to be quietly ambitious. They keep in the background, watching what needs to be done, astutely judging who counts and who does not, and then when they are absolutely sure they are on solid ground, they move in. After such preparation, they are unlikely to make a mistake, but if they do they blame themselves, they are bitterly angry, and they resolve never to repeat their stupidity. Reckless these types are not, but their methods produce good results, and they make steady progress towards their goals.

Aquarius Rat

All Rats are blessed with good brains, but few of them think of themselves as intellectuals. The exceptions are the Rats born under the sign of Aquarius. While being friendly and sociable, the Aquarian Rat also needs time alone to think things through and to study the latest subject that has aroused his interest. Perhaps not so adept at business as most Rats, those born under the sign of Aquarius make up for any deficiency in this department by teeming with good ideas. They are intuitive, very hard working and love to be involved in 'people' projects.

Pisces Rat

Pisces Rats tend to be quieter than their more flamboyant brothers and sisters. They are not drawn to the limelight, and they are not so interested in business as other Rats. In fact, working for other people has little appeal for them, although this is what they often end up doing through want of thinking up a better idea. Should a more enterprising Pisces Rat decide to put his mind to business, however, he will often end up self-employed which suits him extremely well. Having taken the plunge, many a self-employed Pisces Rat surprises himself by doing very well indeed. These types can be amazingly shrewd and intuitive, and once these powers are harnessed to the right career, they progress in leaps and bounds. Pisces Rats tend to do well in spite of themselves.

Ox

Aries Ox

Dynamic Aries brings the Ox a very welcome blast of fire and urgency to stir those methodical bones into faster action. This is a fortunate combination because when the steadfast, industrious, patient qualities of the Ox are combined with quickness of mind and a definite purpose, very little can stand in the way of this subject's progress. Aries Oxen do particularly well in careers where enormous discipline combined with flair and intelligence is required. Many writers are born under this sign as are college lecturers, historical researchers and archaeologists.

Taurus Ox

Oxen are notoriously stubborn creatures but combine them with Taurus the bull and this trait is doubled if not quadrupled. It is not a good idea to box these types into a corner because they will take a stand and refuse to budge even if the house is on fire. Taurean Oxen really will cut off their noses to spite their faces if they feel they have to. Fall out with them and stop talking, and the chances are that the feud will continue to the grave. Yet despite this tendency, Oxen born under the sign of Taurus are not unfriendly types. They are utterly reliable and totally loyal. Family and friends trust them completely. They might be a bit old fashioned and inflexible, but they are lovable too.

Gemini Ox

Chatty Gemini transforms the normally taciturn Ox into a beast which is almost loquacious, at least by the normal standards of these strong silent types. They might even be confident enough to attempt a few jokes, and though humour is not the Oxen's strongpoint, the Gemini Ox can usually produce something respectably amusing if not sidesplittingly funny. Oddly enough, should the Ox set his mind to it and apply his awesome hard work and patience to the subject of humour he might even make a career of it. Some Gemini Oxen have even become accomplished comedians – not simply through natural talent but through sheer hard work and perseverance. More frequently, however, the combination of Gemini with the Ox produces a 'poor man's lawyer' – a highly opinionated individual who can see what's wrong with the government and the legal system and loves to put the world to rights at every opportunity.

Cancer Ox

Oxen born under the sign of Cancer can go very far indeed, not through the application of brainpower although they are by no means unintelligent, but through the skills they have at their fingertips. These subjects are the craftsmen of the universe. Diligent, painstaking, and precise, they are incapable of bodging any practical task they undertake. They will spend hours and hours honing whatever craft has taken their fancy until they reach what looks to others like the peak of perfection. The Cancer Ox won't accept this of course. He can detect the minutest flaw in his own handiwork, but when he is finally forced to hand it over, everyone else is delighted with his efforts. Many artists, potters and sculptors are born under this sign.

Leo Ox

When the Lion of Leo meets the enormous strength of the Ox, the result is a formidable individual, indeed. Annoy or mock these powerful types at your peril. And anyone who dares to pick a fight with the Lion-Ox is likely to come out of it very badly. Most of the time, however, Leo is a friendly lion bringing confidence and a more relaxed attitude to the unbending Ox. These types are more broad-minded and open-hearted than the usual Oxen. They have been known to enjoy parties and once tempted into the limelight they may even find it's not as bad as they feared. In fact, secretly, they're having a ball.

Virgo Ox

Oxen born under the sign of Virgo tend to be very caring types. Though they show their feelings in practical ways and shun sloppy, emotional displays you can rely on an Ox born under Virgo to comfort the sick, help the old folk and notice if anyone in the neighbourhood needs assistance. Florence Nightingale could have been a Virgo Ox. The unsentimental but immensely useful and humane work she did for her sick soldiers is typical of these types. They make excellent nurses and careworkers, forever plumping pillows, smoothing sheets and knowing just the right touches to bring comfort where it is needed. On a personal level, these subjects are inclined to be critical and easily irritated by the small failings of others, but their bark is worse than their bite. Their kindness shines through.

Libra Ox

Generally speaking, the down to earth Ox has little time for putting on the charm. As far as Ox is concerned, people either like you or they don't, and it's not worth worrying about it either way. There's no point in wasting valuable time trying to bend your personality to accommodate the whims of others. Yet when the Ox is born under the sign of Libra, this trait is modified somewhat. Libra people just can't help having charm even if they are Oxen and therefore express that charm more brusquely than usual. The Libran Ox glides effortlessly through life, pleasing others without even realising it. These types are sympathetic and like to help those in need wherever possible. Try to take advantage of their good nature or trick them with an untrue sob story, though, and they will never forgive you.

Scorpio Ox

The typical Ox is notoriously difficult to get to know, and when that Ox happens to be born under the secretive sign of Scorpio, you might as well give up and go home. You'll learn nothing from this creature unless he has some special reason for telling you. Stubborn and silent, these types are very deep indeed; they care nothing for the opinions of others and follow their own impenetrable hearts come what may. However, win the love of one of these unique subjects, and you have a very rare prize indeed. You will unlock a devotion and passion that you have probably never experienced before and will probably never experience again. This is a strangely compelling combination.

Sagittarius Ox

The Ox born under Sagittarius is a more carefree type than his brothers and sisters. Something of the free spirit of the horse touches these subjects, and while there is no chance of them kicking up their heels or doing anything remotely irresponsible, they at least understand these temptations in others and take a more relaxed view of life. The Ox born under Sagittarius is ambitious but independent. These types don't like to be told what to do and are probably more suited to being self-employed than working for others. They are more easy-going than a lot of Oxen and for this reason attract a wider range of friends. Like their Gemini cousins, they might even hazard a joke from time to time. All in all, the Ox born under Sagittarius gets more fun out of life.

Capricorn Ox

Unlike his Sagittarian brother, the Ox born under Capricorn takes himself and life very seriously indeed. These types usually do very well in material terms and often end up in positions of authority; yet if they're not careful, they can look burned out. With good reason. Capricorn Oxen have never learned how to relax, and they see life as a struggle; consequently, for them, it is. Yet they have much to be glad for. They are great savers for a rainy day, and so they never have to worry about unpaid bills, their capacity for hard work is so enormous they can hardly help but achieve a great deal, and before very long they find themselves well off and regarded with respect by everyone in the community. If these types could only manage to unwind, be gentle with themselves and enjoy their success, they could be very happy indeed.

Aquarius Ox

The Ox has never been a flashy sign. These types believe actions speak louder than words, and they like to beaver away without drawing attention to themselves. When this trait is coupled with the slightly introverted though idealistic nature of Aquarius, you get a quiet, complex character who prefers to work behind the scenes and turns modest when the limelight is switched on. Never known for his verbal dexterity, the Ox born under Aquarius can suddenly turn into a persuasive orator when a humanitarian cause sparks unexpected passion. These types make loyal, faithful companions to those who take the trouble to understand them and their intelligence and dogged persistence makes them invaluable as researchers, political assistants and private secretaries.

Pisces Ox

Few Oxen can be described as fey, changeable creatures but those that come the closest will be found under the sign of Pisces. Pisces brings an emotional, artistic quality to the steadfast Ox. These types are loving, faithful and true, yet it is often difficult to guess what they are thinking. Of all the Ox family, Pisces Oxen are likely to be the most moody and yet in many ways also the most creative. The Ox input lends strength and stamina to more delicate Pisces constitutions, enabling them to accomplish far more than other Pisces subjects. Just leave them alone until they're ready to face the world.

Tiger

Aries Tiger

Another combination which could be potentially explosive but, in this case, energetic Aries adds force and power to the Tiger's humanitarian instincts while the Tiger's unworldly nature curbs Aries materialistic streak. These types really could change the world for the better if they put their minds to it. They are kind and thoughtful, and while they might be impatient at times, they quickly regret any harsh words spoken in the heat of the moment.

Taurus Tiger

Taurus Tigers are tremendous achievers. The strength of the zodiac bull added to the fire of the Tiger produces a truly formidable individual who can do almost anything to which he sets his mind. These types often end up making a great deal of money. They have to work hard for all their gains, but this doesn't worry them at all. They also take a great deal of pleasure in spending their hard-earned cash. They like to share what they've got, and this gives them such childish joy that no-one begrudges them their good fortune.

Gemini Tiger

The quicksilver mind of Gemini adds zing and extra flexibility to the Tiger's powerful individualism. These Tigers are blessed with minds which overflow with brilliant ideas. They are creative and often artistic too, so they're capable of wonderful achievements. Their only drawback is that they possess almost too much of a good thing. They have so many ideas that they tend to zoom off at a tangent onto a new task before they have completed the one on which they were working.

Cancer Tiger

These Tigers are immensely clever but a little more retiring than the usual bold, brave terror of the jungle. No Tiger is timid, but Cancer has the effect of quietening the more reckless excesses of the Tiger and allowing a little caution to creep into the blend. They still like a challenge but will opt for something a little less physically demanding than other Tigers. These types are more able to fit into society and tolerate authority better than other Tigers, and for this reason they often do well in their careers.

Leo Tiger

What would you get if you crossed a lion with a tiger? A very wild beast indeed. Some sort of striped wonder of the world no doubt! Leo Tigers certainly make their mark. Tigers are big, beautiful, fearless personalities who crave the limelight and love to be noticed. They believe in doing good deeds, but they like to be noticed doing them. These are not the types of which anonymous benefactors are made. When the Leo Tiger raises money for charity, he likes to make sure the world's press are gathered to record the occasion if at all possible. Yet his heart's in the right place. Let these Tigers have their share of praise, and they will work wonders for others.

Virgo Tiger

The Virgo Tiger is quite a different beast. Virgo accentuates the Tiger's already well-developed sense of justice. These types cannot rest until wrongdoers have got their just deserts. They often go into professions involving the law and the police force. They are immensely self-disciplined and have very high standards. Totally trustworthy and effective, they can sometimes be a little difficult to live with. They are not unkind; it's just that they expect everyone else to be as perfect as they are themselves. Yet Virgo adds attention-to-detail to Tiger's passion to change the world, and the combination creates a character who really could make a lasting difference.

Libra Tiger

Laidback Libra brings quite a different quality to the Tiger. Tiger's intensity is softened by pure Libra charm, and the result is a Tiger of unrivalled compassion and magnetism. Libra Tigers often end up in the caring professions where people flock to them with relief. These Tigers want to help, and Libra gives them the ability to understand just what people need and when. You'd never catch a Libra Tiger helping an old lady across the road who didn't wish to go. Libra Tiger would realise at once that the woman was waiting for a bus, would stand with her to keep her company, help her on when the vehicle arrived and make sure the driver put her off at the right stop. No wonder these Tigers are so well-loved wherever they go.

Scorpio Tiger

Crossing a Scorpion with a Tiger is a very tricky proposition. These types mean well, but they are often misunderstood. Scorpio brings a tremendous depth of feeling to the Tiger's reforming instincts, but this sometimes causes them to put tremendous effort into the wrong causes with alarming results. These types can be very quick-tempered, and they may nurse a grudge for a long time. They never forgive disloyalty, and they never forget. It would be a serious mistake to make an enemy of a Scorpio Tiger – but once this individual becomes a friend, they'll be loyal for life.

Sagittarius Tiger

Another charmer, the Sagittarius Tiger is nevertheless likely to hit the road at the slightest opportunity. These types are wanderers, and no matter how much they seem to enjoy company, they enjoy moving on even more. They can't bear working for other people and do far better being self-employed. The travel industry would suit them perfectly. Impossible to cage in or pin down – don't even try – the only way to have a happy relationship with a Sagittarius Tiger is to make them feel free at all times.

Capricorn Tiger

Steady Capricorn lends a prudent touch to the impulsive Tiger, and these types are the Tigers most likely to stop and think before rushing off to save the rain forest. They still enjoy improving the world, but they check travel arrangements, make sure they have got sufficient funds and do a bit of research online first. These are not party animals. While they enjoy company, they prefer serious discussion to frivolous small talk and much as they enjoy travel, they appreciate the comfort of home. These Tigers like to develop their theories from the depths of their favourite armchair beside their own cosy hearth.

Aquarius Tiger

When idealistic Aquarius meets idealistic Tiger, you have to hang onto that long tiger tail to keep these subjects, feet on the ground. These types really do have their heads in the clouds and are totally unpredictable. Once a worthwhile cause presents itself, they will rush off immediately without a thought to the consequences. Convention is of no interest to them. They couldn't care less what other people think. They go through life guided entirely by a strong inner sense of right and wrong. If it's right, they know it without a shadow of a doubt; if it's wrong, they will not do it no matter what anyone says. This attitude can get them into a lot of trouble, but other signs sneakily admire their courage. People may not agree with Aquarius Tiger, but no one can doubt his integrity.

Pisces Tiger

One of Tiger's failings is a tendency to be indecisive without warning, and this trait is heightened in Pisces Tigers. These types are anxious to do the right thing; it's just that sometimes it's very difficult to know what that right thing is. There are so many alternatives. Pisces Tiger is kind and gentle and apt to get sentimental at times. They want to save the world, but they'd like someone alongside to help them – though not too many. Despite their indecision, they usually end up heading in the right direction in the end. Yet, even when they've achieved a great deal, they still agonise over whether they could have done even more.

Rabbit

Aries Rabbit

This is a very dynamic Rabbit. When powerful Aries injects a streak of energy into that cultured Rabbit personality, the result is a wonderfully clever individual who glides effortlessly to success. Although at times Aries Rabbit has an attack of over-cautiousness, these types are usually bolder than the average bunny and achieve much where other Rabbits might run away. Occasionally, these Rabbits will even take a gamble, and this is worthwhile as it usually pays off for them.

Taurus Rabbit

The Taurus Rabbit really does feel his home is his castle. He is not unduly interested in his career, but he is likely to turn his home into an art form. Brilliant entertainers, these types guarantee their lucky guests will enjoy all the creature comforts possible. They often marry later in life than average, but when they do, they work at the relationship. Providing they choose another home bird, they are likely to be very happy.

Gemini Rabbit

All Rabbits are natural diplomats, but the Gemini Rabbit really is the star of them all. So skilled a communicator is this creature, so expert at people management that a career in the diplomatic service, politics, psychology or even advertising is an option. Never lost for words, these types can persuade anyone to do almost anything. As a result, they are usually very successful. Once they harness their enviable skills to a worthwhile career, they can go far.

Cancer Rabbit

Cancer Rabbits are gentle, kindly souls. They like to be surrounded by pleasant company and prefer to have few demands put upon them. They don't really take to business life and find many professions too abrasive. On the other hand, they find working for themselves too stressful a venture to be considered seriously. They are happiest in a peaceful, routine environment where they can make steady progress, but really their hearts are at home. Home is where they express themselves.

Leo Rabbit

Leo Rabbits, on the other hand, are usually very popular with a wide circle of friends. Extrovert Leo gives Rabbit a strong dose of confidence and flair, and when these qualities are added to Rabbit's people skills, a radiant, magnetic individual is born. Leo Rabbits adore parties where they shine. They are always elegant and beautifully turned out and have a knack of putting others at their ease. These Rabbits climb the ladder of success very quickly.

Virgo Rabbit

Virgo Rabbits have a lot on their minds. The natural cautiousness of the Rabbit is heightened by the same quality in Virgo, and these Rabbits tend to be born worriers. They are masters of detail but, unfortunately, this often leads them to make mountains out of molehills. They are very talented creatures but too often fail to make the best use of their gifts because they spend so much time worrying about all the things that could go wrong. If they can learn to relax and take the odd risk now and then, they will go far.

Libra Rabbit

Art-loving Libra blends easily into the cultured sign of the Rabbit. These types love to learn more about beautiful things, and they like to share their knowledge with others. They are so good with people that they can convey information effortlessly and make the dullest subject sound interesting. These types are often gifted teachers and lecturers though they would find difficult inner-city schools too traumatic. Give these types willing and interested pupils, and they blossom.

Scorpio Rabbit

Rabbits tend to be discreet people, and Scorpio Rabbits are the most tight-lipped of the lot. Scorpio Rabbits have a lot of secrets, and they enjoy keeping them. It gives them a wonderful feeling of superiority to think that they know things others don't. They have many secret ambitions too, and they don't like to speak of them in case others are pessimistic and pour scorn on their plans. So, it is the Scorpio Rabbit who is most likely to surprise everyone by suddenly reaching an amazing goal that no-one even knew he was aiming for.

Sagittarius Rabbit

Sporty Sagittarius brings a whole new dimension to the art-loving Rabbit. Rabbits are often indoor creatures, but Sagittarian Rabbits are much more adventurous in the open air than the usual bunny. They are sensuous and fun and attract many friends. They are also versatile and can turn their hands to several different careers if necessary. They like to get out and about more than most Rabbits and they are usually very successful.

Capricorn Rabbit

Capricorn Rabbits are great family folk. They firmly believe the family is the bedrock of life, and they work hard to keep their relations happy and together. The Capricorn Rabbit home is the centre of numerous clan gatherings throughout the year and weddings, birthdays, anniversaries and christenings are very important to them. Capricorn Rabbit will never forget the dates. These types are particularly interested in the past and will enjoy researching a family tree going back generations. If it ever crosses their minds that the rest of the tribe seems to leave all the donkey work to Capricorn Rabbit, he'd never say so. And, in truth, he doesn't really mind. There's nothing he loves more than having his family around him.

Aquarius Rabbit

The Aquarius Rabbit is a contradictory creature being both cautious and curious at the same time. These types crave security and love, and yet they have a great longing to find out more about everything around them. Fascinated by art, science and new inventions they love to potter about in book shops and tinker in the shed at home. Once they get an idea in their head, they can't rest until they have experimented with it, frequently forgetting to eat while they work. They need love and understanding.

Pisces Rabbit

The Pisces Rabbit is another bunny who needs a lot of understanding. Often gifted artistically they can sometimes be stubborn and awkward for no apparent reason. Yet when they are in the right frame of mind, they can charm the birds off the trees. It takes them a long time to make a friend, but when they do, it is a friend for life. The Pisces Rabbit home is full of beautiful things, and these subjects love to invite their most trusted friends to come and enjoy the magic.

Dragon

Aries Dragon

The Dragon is already a powerful sign, but when the lively influence of Aries is added, you have a positively devastating individual. These are the types that others either love or loathe. Strong, confident people can cope happily with the Aries Dragon, but more timid souls are terrified.

The Aries Dragon himself is quite unaware of the reaction he causes. He goes busily on his way oblivious of the earthquakes all around him. These types have to guard against arrogance, particularly since they have quite a lot to be arrogant about. They also have a tendency to get bored easily and move on to new projects without completing the old, which is a pity since they can accomplish much if they persevere.

Taurus Dragon

There is something magnificent about the Taurus Dragon. Large, expansive types, they move easily around the social scene spreading bonhomie wherever they go. Not the most sensitive of individuals, they find it difficult to assess the moods of others and assume everyone else feels the same way they do. Should it be brought to their attention that someone is unhappy, however, they will move heaven and earth to cheer them up. These types are reliable and conscientious and always keep their promises.

Gemini Dragon

Dragons may not have the quickest minds in the Chinese zodiac, but Gemini Dragons are speedier than most. They are jovial types with a brilliant sense of humour. In fact, they can cleverly joke others into doing what they want. These types have no need for physical force to get their own way; they use laughter instead. At times, Gemini Dragons can be almost devious, which is unusual for a Dragon but nobody really minds their schemes. They give everyone such a good time on the way it's worth doing what they want for the sheer entertainment.

Cancer Dragon

Cautious Cancer and flamboyant Dragon make a surprisingly good combination. Cancer holds Dragon back where he might go too far, while Dragon endows the Crab with exuberance and style. These types like to help others make the most of themselves, but they are also high achievers in their own right. Without upsetting anyone, Cancer Dragons tend to zoom to the top faster than most.

Leo Dragon

This Dragon is so dazzling you need sunglasses to look at him. The proud, glorious Lion combined with the magnificent Dragon is an extraordinary combination, and it's fortunate it only comes around once every twelve years. Too many of such splendid creatures would be hard to take. Leo Dragons really do have star quality, and they know it. They demand to be the centre of attention and praise is like oxygen to them

– they can't live without it. Yet they have generous hearts, and if anyone is in trouble, Leo Dragon will be the first to rush to their assistance.

Virgo Dragon

Unusually for a Dragon, the Virgo variety can get quite aggressive if crossed, but this doesn't often happen as very few people would dare take on such a daunting beast. These types are immensely clever in business. They steadily add acquisition to shrewd acquisition until they end up seriously rich. They are wilier than most Dragons who have a surprisingly naive streak, and they make the most of it. These types just can't help becoming successful in whatever they undertake.

Libra Dragon

Dragons are not usually too bothered about trifles such as fine clothes and wallpaper. In fact, some older, more absent-minded Dragons have been known to go shopping in their slippers having forgotten to take them off. The exception is the Dragon born under the sign of Libra. These types are more down to earth and see the sense in putting on a good show for others. They take the trouble to choose smart clothes and keep them looking that way at all times. They are also more intuitive and are not easily fooled by others.

Scorpio Dragon

Handling money is not a Dragon strong point, but the Scorpio variety has more ability in this direction than most. Scorpio Dragons enjoy amassing cash. Rather like their legendary namesakes who hoard treasure in their lairs, Scorpio Dragons like to build substantial nest-eggs and keep them close at hand where they can admire them regularly. These types can also be a little stingy financially, not out of true meanness but simply because they don't like to see their carefully guarded heap diminish in size. Once they understand the importance of a purchase, however, they can be just as generous as their brothers and sisters.

Sagittarius Dragon

When Sagittarius joins the Dragon, the combination produces a real livewire, a true daredevil. The antics of the Sagittarius Dragon, when young, will give their mothers nightmares and later drive their partners to drink. These types can't resist a challenge, particularly a dangerous one. They will climb mountain peaks, leap off cliffs on a hang-glider and try a spot of bungee-jumping to enliven a dull moment. It's no good expecting these types to sit down with a good book; they just can't keep still. However, surrounded by friends, dashing from one perilous venture to the next, the Sagittarius Dragon is one of the happiest people around.

Capricorn Dragon

The Capricorn Dragon looks back at his Sagittarian brother in horror. He simply can't understand the need for such pranks. Being Dragons, these types are bold, but the influence of Capricorn ensures that they are never foolhardy. They look before they leap and occasionally miss a good deal because they stop to check the fine print. They are not the most intuitive of creatures, but show them a needy soul and they will efficiently do whatever's necessary to help. The Capricorn Dragon is a highly effective creature.

Aquarius Dragon

Happy go lucky types, the Aquarius Dragons are usually surrounded by people. Honest and hardworking, they will put in just as much effort for very little cash as they will for a great deal. If someone asks them to do a job and they agree to do it, they will move heaven and earth to fulfil their obligations even if it is not in their best interests to do so. However, they're not suited to routine, and if a task doesn't interest them, they will avoid it at all costs no matter how well paid it might be. Not particularly interested in money for its own sake, these types are sociable and easy to get along with. They are often highly talented in some way.

Pisces Dragon

Pisces Dragons, on the other hand, are surprisingly good with cash. Despite their often vague, good-humoured exteriors these types have excellent financial brains and seem to know just what to do to increase their savings. They are first in the queue when bargains are to be found, and they seem to sense what the next money-making trend is going to be before anyone else has thought of it. These types often end up quite wealthy and excel, particularly, in artistic fields.

CHAPTER 17: CREATE A WONDERFUL YEAR

By now, you should have a pretty good idea of the main zodiac influences on your lifestyle and personality, according to Chinese astrology. But how is 2025 going to shape up for you in general? Well, that largely depends on how cleverly you play your hand.

Snake years are traditionally regarded as calmer, yet with mysterious undercurrents. Change is occurring but subtly, so few notice it until the transformation is complete. Yet the Snake also has the ability to strike suddenly, taking people by surprise, and the same is true in Snake years. Every year brings its changes, of course, but in Snake years these tend to evolve gradually and apparently by accident. Stand by though for complete surprises that come out of the blue, catching everyone off guard.

The key point is that – according to Chinese astrology – everything should be in balance. So, after the forceful energy that tore through last year like a tornado during the Year of the Dragon, the world is now longing for a chance to ease up. After 12 months of struggling to assimilate the complicated twists and turns of the Dragon's drama, we're now ready for something a little more thoughtful and introspective.

In 2025, the emphasis will be on wisdom, diplomacy, behind-the-scenes agreements, and delving into hidden truths. Treachery and backstabbing may be revealed and punished. And a new interest in mysticism and magic could be unleashed.

Some signs will find these conditions more comfortable than others. Zodiac creatures that prefer to leap straight in, to act first and ask questions later, could find the slower yet picky 2025 vibe irritating. Reflective, naturally cautious, detail-oriented signs will thrive. Yet, whichever group you belong to, as long as you're prepared – and you know what you might be up against – you can develop a strategy to ride those waves like a world-class surfer.

Sit back and rely on good fortune alone, because it's a terrific year for your sign, and you could snatch failure from the jaws of success. Navigate any stormy seas with skill and foresight if it's not such a sunny year for your sign, and you'll sail on to fulfil your dreams.

This is always true in any year, but doubly so when the wily Snake is in charge. Be smart, careful, and prepared to dig deep, and the Snake will smile on you. So, no matter what zodiac sign you were born under, the luck of the Snake will help you… if you help yourself.

The future is not set in stone.

Chinese astrology is used very much like a weather forecast. You check out the likely conditions you'll encounter on your journey through the year, and plan your route and equipment accordingly. Some signs might need a parasol, sunscreen, and sandals; others might require stout walking boots and rain gear.

Yet, properly prepared, both will end up in a good place at the end of the trip.

Finally, it's said that if you feel another sign has a much better outlook than you this year, you can carry a small symbol of that animal with you (in the form of a piece of jewellery, perhaps, or a tiny charm in your pocket or bag) and their good luck will rub off on you. Does it work? For some, maybe, but there's certainly no harm in trying.

Other Books from the Publisher

Linda Dearsley – *the author of this book* **–** was Doris Stokes' ghost.

Well, more accurately, she was the ghost-writer for Doris Stokes and worked with her for 10 years to produce 7 books, detailing the great lady's life.

In Voices Everywhere, Linda shines a light on her time working with Doris, right from the very early days when Doris was doing private readings in her Fulham flat, to filling the London Palladium and Barbican night after night, to subsequent fame outside the UK. Throughout all this, Doris Stokes never became anyone other than who she was: a kind, generous, and down-to-earth woman with an extraordinary gift, and a fondness for a nice cup of tea. January 6th, 2020, would have been Doris' 100th birthday.

Following Doris' death, Linda chronicles how cynics tried to torpedo the Stokes legacy with accusations of cheating and dishonesty, but how those closest to Doris never believed she was anything other than genuine.

In turn, as the months and years rolled by, more and more intriguing people crossed Linda's path, each with their own unexplainable power, and Doris never seemed far away. From the palmist who saw pictures in people's hands, to the couple whose marriage was predicted by Doris, and the woman who believes she captures departed spirits on camera – the mysterious world of the paranormal, and Doris Stokes' place within it, continues to unfold.

Karina Collins is an acclaimed Tarot reader who has helped people, from all walks of life, to better understand their lives' journeys.

Now, she is on a mission to help you take control of your life – through the power of Tarot – to better explore and understand your purpose and destiny.

Do you have questions about now and your future? Perhaps about making more money, or whether love is on the horizon, or whether you will become happier? Do you want to steer your life in a direction that brings success, pleasure, and fulfilment? Well, Tarot is a means to help you do exactly that! Used for centuries, it provides a powerful tool for unlocking knowledge, divining the future, and delivering shortcuts to the lives we desire.

In this full-colour top-rated book, Karina provides explanations and insights into the full 78-card Tarot deck, how to phrase questions most effectively, real-world sample readings, why seemingly scary cards represent opportunities for growth and triumph, and more.

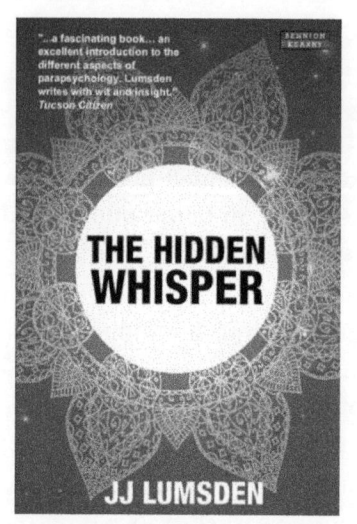

A paranormal puzzle smoulders in the desert heat of southern Arizona. At the home of Jack and Chloe Monroe, a written message "Leave Now" appears then disappears, a candle in an empty room mysteriously lights itself, and – most enigmatically – an unidentifiable ethereal whisper begins to permeate the house. What was once simply strange now feels sinister. What once seemed a curiosity now seems terrifying.

Dr. Luke Jackson, a British Parapsychologist visiting family nearby, is asked to investigate and quickly finds himself drawn deeper into the series of unexplained events. Time is against him. He has just one week to understand and resolve the poltergeist case before he must depart Arizona.

The Hidden Whisper is the acclaimed paranormal thriller, written by real-life parapsychologist Dr. JJ Lumsden, which offers a rare opportunity to enter the intriguing world of parapsychology through the eyes of Luke Jackson. The fictional narrative is combined with extensive endnotes and references that cover Extra Sensory Perception, Psychokinesis, Haunts, Poltergeists, Out of Body Experiences, and more. If you thought parapsychology was like Ghostbusters – think again…

"This book works on many levels, an excellent introduction to the concepts current in the field of parapsychology… at best you may learn something new, and at worst you'll have read a witty and well-written paranormal detective story" Parascience.

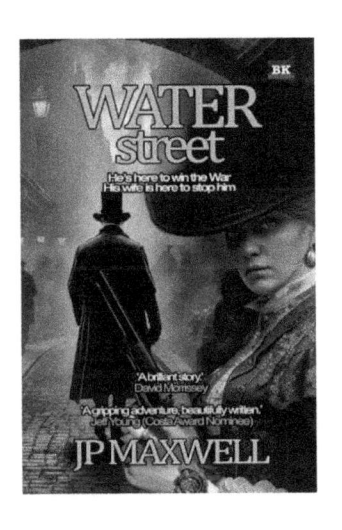

WATER street

He's here to win the War
His wife is here to stop him

'A brilliant story.'
David Morrissey

'A gripping adventure, beautifully written.'
Gell Young (Costa Award Nominee)

JP MAXWELL

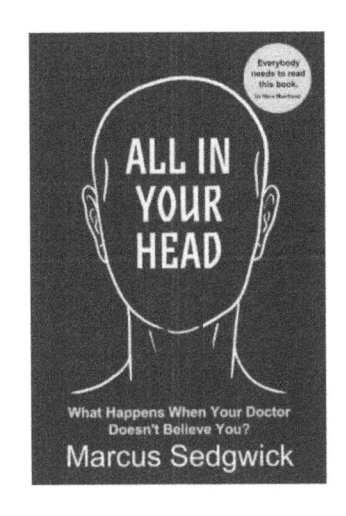

Everybody needs to read this book.

ALL IN YOUR HEAD

What Happens When Your Doctor Doesn't Believe You?

Marcus Sedgwick

STEER INTO THE SKID

AN 8-STEP GUIDE TO MANAGING YOUR CANCER JOURNEY

Ted Garratt

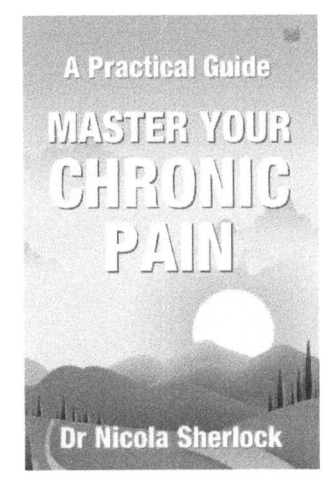

A Practical Guide

MASTER YOUR CHRONIC PAIN

Dr Nicola Sherlock

www.ingramcontent.com/pod-product-compliance
Ingram Content Group UK Ltd.
Pitfield, Milton Keynes, MK11 3LW, UK
UKHW040725020125
453205UK00005B/367